SERVANTHOOD LEADERSHIP
Jesus' Model

Dr. Freddy P S Olela

First published by Busybird Publishing 2025

Copyright © 2025 Dr. Freddy P S Olela

ISBN:
Print: 978 1 738198 90 0

This work is copyright. Apart from any use permitted under the *Copyright Act 1968*, no part of this publication may be reproduced, stored in a retrieval system or transmitted in any form or by any means, electronic, mechanical, photocopying, recording or otherwise, without the prior written permission of Dr. Freddy P S Olela.

The information in this book is based on the author's experiences and opinions. The author and publisher disclaim responsibility for any adverse consequences, which may result from use of the information contained herein. Permission to use any external content has been sought by the author. Any breaches will be rectified in further editions of the book.

Layout and typesetting: Busybird Publishing

Busybird Publishing
2/118 Para Road
Montmorency, Victoria
Australia 3094
www.busybird.com.au

DEDICATION

I am infinitely grateful to the Lord for the help in giving me my wife Billie Malaika Olela: A woman according to the Book of Proverbs 31.

Thank you, Billie, for your unconditional support, patience and encouragement.

My thanks also go to my late Grandmother, Elongo Ehomo Pauline, and my mother, Marie Therese Manga Olela, who shaped my character since my childhood with the "Never Die" attitude.

Last but not least, I am grateful to my precious children: Zoe; Shekinah; Joshua; Kenaniah; Malaika and Israelah Olela you guys are such a blessing may my God continue to keep and bless you in Jesus' name.

At His Service,

Doctor Freddy P S Olela

Contents

Preface	1
1. Introduction	3
2. What is Leadership?	5
TO CROSS A RIVER	10
1. AN ALL EMCOMPASSING DEFINITION	13
2. THERE ARE THREE ESSENTIAL PARTS TO THIS LEADERSHIP DEFINITION:	16
2.1. THE LEADER ESTABLISHES THE DIRECTION	16
2.2. THE LEADER ALIGNS THE PEOPLE IN THAT DIRECTION	17
2.3. THE LEADER MOTIVATES AND INSPIRES THE PEOPLE TO IMPLEMENT AND ACHIEVE THE VISION	18
3. JESUS FULFILMENT OF THREE PARTS OF LEADERSHIP	18
3. THE WORLDVIEW ON LEADERSHIP	20
Key Trait 1: You must have a vision.	22
Key Trait 2: You must have passion.	23
Key Trait 3: You must learn to be a great decision maker.	23
Key Trait 4: You must be a team builder.	24
Key Trait 5: You must have character.	25
3.1 DIRECTION FOR THE FUTURE	30
3.2 DISCERNMENT OF PEOPLE	31
3.3 THE SITUATIONAL LEADERSHIP MODEL	35
3.4 REVIEW OF LEADERSHIP THEORY	38
a. GREAT MAN THEORIES	38
b. TRAIT THEORIES	38
c. BEHAVIOURIST THEORIES	38
d. CONTINGENCY THEORY	38
e. TRANSACTIONAL THEORY	39
f. TRANSFORMATIONAL THEORY	39
The Contingency or Situational School	43
3.5 SITUATIONAL LEADERSHIP	49
a. THE BENEFITS OF SITUATIONAL LEADERSHIP	50
3.6 THE THREE LEVELS OF LEADERSHIP	52
a. PUBLIC LEADERSHIP	55
b. PRIVATE LEADERSHIP	56
c. PERSONAL LEADERSHIP	57

3.7 LEADERSHIP PRESENCE	59
LINK WITH AUTHENTIC LEADERSHIP AND SERVANT LEADERSHIP	61
SHARED LEADERSHIP	62
CORE LEADERSHIP THEORIES	64
THE FOUR CORE THEORY GROUPS	65
EFFECTIVE LEADERSHIP STYLES	68
AUTHORITARIAN LEADER HIGH TASK, LOW RELATIONSHIP	68
TEAM LEADER HIGH TASK, HIGH RELATIONSHIP	69
WHAT IS WORLDVIEW AND HOW DOES IT AFFECT LEADERSHIP?	69
A MODEL OF THE WORLD	**71**
EXPLANATION	71
FUTUROLOGY	71
VALUES	71
ACTION	72
KNOWLEDGE	72
BUILDING BLOCKS	72
WHAT IS A CHRISTIAN WORLDVIEW?	**73**
THE WORLDVIEW OUTCOME	75
4. WHAT IS SERVANT LEARDERSHIP?	**77**
THE PRIMARY CHARACTERISTIC OF SERVANT LEADERSHIP	81
7 THINGS GREAT LEADERS ALWAYS DO BUT MERE MANAGERS ALWAYS FEAR	94
5. WHAT JESUS HAS TO SAY ON LEADERSHIP	**97**
JESUS SERVED HUMBLY	102
JESUS SERVED OBEDIENTLY	102
CHARACTERISTICS OF JESUS AS A SERVANT	103
JESUS SERVED LOVINGLY	106
JESUS DESCRIBES HIMSELF AS A SERVANT IN HIS TEACHING	107
THE APOSTLE PAUL DESCRIBES JESUS AS A SERVANT	108
JESUS PRAISES THE CHARACTER OF A TRUSTING SERVANT	109
A DIFFERENT LEADERSHIP STYLE	111
WHAT LEADING WITH THE TOWEL MEANS	113
JESUS DIFFERENT LEADERSHIP VALUES	115
HOW WAS JESUS ABLE TO HUMBLE HIMSELF?	120
CONCLUSION	**125**
BIBLIOGRAPHY	**127**

Preface

"It was an honour to endorse Dr Freddy Olela's latest book "Servanthood Leadership: Jesus' Model". Dr Freddy demonstrates what he preaches in Australia, Africa and around the world. He lives what he teaches. I have long been a lover of leadership books and training materials. There is a lot of research that has gone into this book with ample wealth from many great leaders.

Most of us will be able to connect instantly with the examples of those who have shaped our biblical and secular mindsets over many years.

However, you will no doubt also be blessed by a few names you don't know. Ultimately, the reader is bombarded with leadership truth from every angle.

For example, James Scouller's teaching on 'Leadership presence'. I quote: "The best leaders usually have something beyond their behaviour - something distinctive that commands attention/wins people's trust and enables them to lead successfully." These gems can be found throughout the book.

But what blesses beyond the examples of men and women in this book is the consistent revelation Dr Freddy brings of Jesus Christ the servant leader who led with a towel.

Jesus is majestically glorified through scripture in this book as the servant leader. Dr Freddy teaches with heart and passion. His call to train empowers and releases leaders.

Pastor Malcolm Macleod
Equip Church International,
Melbourne, Australia

1. Introduction

Have you ever thought about the leadership style of Jesus Christ? There has never been anyone who has had an influence on the world the same way Jesus had. He began his ministry with a small group of men whom he equipped to change the world. Jesus' strategy of leading did not focus on status, prosperity, control, technics nor power. Jesus' plan, from the very beginning of his ministry, was to be a servant leader. The kind of leadership style Jesus had is a strategy that will benefit any association, business, humanity group or audience.

So, in this book I want us to learn the principle of transformative leadership by studying how Jesus led.

No matter what leadership field a person serves in, whether leading a family, a church, a civic organisation, or a company, adopting the leadership example of Jesus will make that person more effective and productive. One of the definitions of Leadership is influence, and there has been no leader who has had greater influence on the world than Jesus Christ. The lessons from his leadership style are practical and learnable skills that anyone can still apply today.

Men and women in search of excellence in developing their leadership abilities will find much to aid their quest in this close look at Jesus the greatest leader who ever lived. The more we understand the Bible, the more evident it becomes that everything about effective leadership Jesus did to perfection. He is simply the greatest leadership role model of all time. How to lead like Jesus?

2. What is Leadership?

Before answering that question, let's first state what leadership is not...(Kruse).

a. Leadership has nothing to do with seniority or one's position in the hierarchy of a company. Many people talk about a company's leadership while referring to the senior most executives in the organisation. They are just that, senior executives. Leadership doesn't automatically happen when you reach a certain pay bracket. Hopefully you find it there, but there are no guarantees.

b. Leadership is not a title and has nothing to do with titles. Like the point above, just because you have a title, doesn't automatically make you fit to be a 'leader'. You don't need a title to lead. In fact, you can be a leader in your place of worship, your neighbourhood, in your family, all areas of your life without having any title.

c. Leadership has nothing to do with personal attributes. While using the word 'leader' most people think of a domineering, take-charge charismatic individual who take charge. We often think of icons from history like Winston Churchill or President Kadhafi, but leadership isn't an adjective. We don't need extroverted charismatic traits to practice leadership; those with charisma don't automatically lead.

d. Leadership isn't management. This is the big one. Leadership and management are not synonymous. You may have twenty people in your responsibility. That is good, hopefully you are a good manager. While still acknowledging that good management is needed and managers need to plan, measure, monitor, coordinate, solve, hire, fire, and so many other things, we assert that the typical difference between them is that managers manage things while leaders lead people.

Let's see how some of the most respected business thinkers of our time define leadership, and let's consider what's wrong with their definitions.

> Peter Drucker: "The only definition of a leader is someone who has followers."

Really? This kind of statement (tautology) is so simplistic it is dangerous. A new Army Captain is put in command of two hundred soldiers. He never leaves his room or utters a word to the men and women in his unit. Perhaps routine orders are given through a subordinate. By default, his troops must 'follow' orders. Is the Captain really a leader? Commander yes, leader no. Drucker is of course a brilliant thinker of modern business, but his definition of a leader is too simple.

> Warren Bennis: "Leadership is the capacity to translate vision into reality."

Every spring you have a vision for a garden, and with lots of work carrots and tomatoes become a reality. Are you a leader? No, you are a gardener. Bennis' definition seems to have forgotten 'others'.

> Bill Gates: "As we look ahead into the next century, leaders will be those who empower others."

This definition includes 'others', and empowerment is a good thing. But to what aim? We've seen many empowering 'others" lives, from rioting hooligans to Google workers who were so misaligned with the rest of the company they found themselves unemployed. Gates' definition lacks the parts about goal or vision. (Bradberry)

Some current brief definitions of leadership are:

- Leadership is relationship.
- Leadership is influence.
- Leadership is vision.
- Leadership is transformation.
- Leadership is empowerment.
- Leadership is personal responsibility.
- Leadership is decision-making.
- Leadership is team building.
- Leadership is change or managing change.
- Leadership is culture.

- Leadership is motivation.
- Leadership is persuasion.
- Leadership is creativity.
- Leadership is self-management.
- Leadership is communication.
- Leadership is character or integrity.
- Leadership is credibility.
- Leadership is trust.
- Leadership is modelling.
- Leadership is servanthood.

These are all good definitions of certain aspects of leadership but none of them is a sufficient definition overall. They are all too brief, too limited and inadequate. The broad definition Webber gave in his book Spirit Built Leadership is: "A leader helps someone move from where he is now to somewhere else" (Webber 6).

In addition, it is probably somewhere he would not go on his own. That is why he needs a leader. Leaders are necessary to help people move. People need leaders, or else they tend to stay in the same place.

Moses said to the Lord, "May the Lord, the God of the spirits of all mankind, appoint a man over this community to go out and come in before them, one who will lead them out and bring them in, so the Lord's people will not be like sheep without a shepherd" (Num. 27:15-17).

Jesus went through all the towns and villages, teaching in their synagogues, preaching the good news of the Kingdom, and healing every disease and sickness. When he saw the crowds, he had compassion for them, because they were harassed and helpless, like sheep without a shepherd. Then he said to his disciples, "The harvest is plentiful, but the workers are few. Ask the Lord of the harvest, therefore, to send out workers into his harvest field." (Matt.9:35-38).

Without leaders, people are like "sheep without a shepherd" - they wander aimlessly around accomplishing very little. A leader helps someone **move from where he is now to somewhere else**.

Hopefully, the "somewhere else" is somewhere better than where he is now. This is one difference between a good leader and a bad one. Good leaders help people move to better places; bad leaders take people to worse places - they are effective leaders, but they are bad!

The lack of leadership is why so many people are not progressing in their lives. Many churches have great pastors, but many pastors aren't leaders. They are maintaining; they are taking care of the people in their church, but they are not leading. They are not helping their people to move anywhere.

The people are only surviving; they are not fulfilling God's purposes. Certainly, the people do need to be taken care of but that is not enough. They also need to go somewhere. They need to mature and to fulfil God's purposes.

The scarcest resource in the church today is the kind of leadership capable of leading the people to fulfil God's purposes.

Why is there a lack of leadership in so many churches today?

Many men in leadership positions simply don't have a leadership orientation or calling and many more who are called leaders are not sufficiently equipped in leadership. Many men who are leaders have no time for the future because they're too absorbed in the present. Moreover, the lack of leadership is why many businesses stagnate. They may be good at what they do, but they are not keeping up with the business environment that is fast changing. Many businesses are being left behind because of a lack of leadership. The lack of leadership is also why many families do not fulfil the purposes of God for their lives. The lack of leadership is why nations, who are otherwise rich in resources, stagnate. As a leader, you help someone move somewhere else, somewhere they probably would not have gone by themselves. That is leadership. Thus, leaders build bridges:

> From here to a better place.
>
> From the present to the future.
>
> From potential to fulfilment.
>
> From vision to experience.
>
> From anticipation to realization.

TO CROSS A RIVER

If there were only a few people who needed to move, then that few could swim. Boats could help a few more move from the present to the future. But if we want many people to make the move, we need a leader to build a bridge.

Let's look closely to this definition:

A leader:

> This may be in any context of church, family, business, government, or education. Moreover, it may be at any level throughout any organization.
>
> The leader may be good or bad. There is both good and bad leadership. A good leader leads people somewhere good; a bad leader leads people somewhere bad. A leader leads you; he moves you; he takes you somewhere different from where you are now, that place may be either good or bad. Hitler, Stalin and Mussolini were all extraordinary leaders. In fact, they were very effective leaders. They moved many people great distances. However, they were bad leaders because where they moved the people to was bad.

Helps:

The good leader 'helps' people move. He does not make them move. This is how he does it:

The leader is at the front – calling to the people, "Look! Here's the vision!" "Here's where we can go!" "Here's what we can accomplish!" "Wow!" "Let's go!"

The leader is behind – picking the people up when they fall, encouraging them, "you can do it!"

The leader is on the side – showing the way to the people; "Watch! Here's how to do it! Here's the path to walk in to get where we're going."

Someone:

The leader must have followers. A person may be a great speaker, writer, scientist, inventor, musician or artist, but if no one is following him, he is not a "leader." These followers must be people. Leadership involves people. It is distinct from administrative paperwork, committee meetings, planning activities, or writing sermons.

Move:

Leadership involves movement; leadership involves change. Leaders must be willing to follow God when the cloud moves and to repeatedly let go of old ideas and old ways of doing things and adopt new and better ones.

Moreover, they must be able to help their followers generate the high levels of enthusiasm needed to accomplish change. For the change to succeed, many people across the entire organization must move, but the leader is the one who often starts the movement or gives it direction and momentum.

Speaking of change, we do not mean leaders will change orthodox doctrine or the eternal truths of the word of God.

Many pastors would make quantum leaps ahead in their leadership if they would simply get out of their studies and touch people with the word of God.

Some spiritual leaders resist the idea of change because of their commitment to the unchanging Word of God. However, you can take a bottle of pure water and pour it into a variety of very different containers without the water itself being changed at all. In the same way, the eternal truths of God can be expressed in many ways and in different forms. Sometimes, however, these forms become chains or straitjackets. They stifle people and make people ineffective in their ministries to others. It is these external forms, structures, processes, habits, ministry strategies, etc. that God often wants to change.

From where he is now:

> The leader first understands where the people are now. Realistically, he examines the current state. He defines the need for change; he is not interested merely in change for its own sake. The leader must understand his people, their needs, conditions, circumstances, aspirations, and capacities:

Be sure you know the condition of your flocks, give careful attention to your herds; (Prov. 27:23)

My sheep listen to my voice; I know them, and they follow me. (John 10:27 NIV)

> The proposed change must serve the people, not merely the leader's own personal ambitions. Moreover, a good

leader is deeply concerned with maintaining social harmony between the people throughout the change.

To somewhere else:

> After defining where the people are now, the leader then defines where they could and/or should go. He also defines the potential, the opportunity, the vision for the future or the solution to a major current problem. Then he defines how they will get there, the path, the broad plan. Then he says, "Let's go!" and leads them there. Along the way he encourages them to continue through the inevitable setbacks and disappointments until finally they reach their goal (Zaleznik).

1. AN ALL EMCOMPASSING DEFINITION

From now on we know that a leader helps someone move from where he is now to somewhere else.

This definition of leadership encompasses all the other short definitions we first mentioned:

Leadership is relationship: It is a relational activity involving people. Leadership is not bookwork, budgeting or accounting – leaders interact with people, keeping the social fabric of the organization healthy. They maintain harmony as they help the people move and fulfil God's purposes.

Leadership is influence: The leader influences people to make the move.

Leadership is vision: The leader sees and then presents the compelling vision of where the move is to.

Leadership is transformation: In the process of making the move, everyone involved is transformed.

Leadership is empowerment: Good leaders empower the people to take responsibility and ownership of their move. Leaders believe in people and want them to fulfil their purposes in God.

Leadership is personal responsibility: Rather than hunting for flaws in any matter or blaming others and influences or events, the leader takes personal responsibility to move each person and encourage personal responsibility for the move to the desired future.

Leadership is decision-making: Leaders have the courage and skills to make the move necessary, and sometimes make hard decisions regarding the move.

Leadership is team building: good leaders realise they cannot do it all on their own; so, they build an empowered team that will lead the people through the move. It takes a team to build a bridge from the present to the future.

Leadership is change or managing change: Leadership always involves change. This is the move itself to somewhere better.

Leadership is culture: Organisational culture is the set of shared beliefs, values and behaviours. This is how the leader leads - by shaping the organization's culture. This is one of the main things a leader does. The leader is a social architect. He designs and builds social structures within his organization. Those characteristics did not just fall into place by themselves. The leaders built this culture whether intentionally or otherwise.

Leadership is communication: It involves communication of the vision, the process and then encouragement and clarification along the way. For communication to be effective, it must have three characteristics:

a. Clarity

b. Passion

c. Integrity

Clear communication will show the people where to go and how to get there. Passionate communication will help the people want to go; and then integrity will mean they will trust you enough to follow you there.

Without the ability to engage, convince, and inspire others in large groups in public and with individuals in private settings, leaders will find it difficult to enlist people in their cause.

Leadership is motivation: The leader must motivate the followers or else they will never move. He should not do this through guilt, fear or force. The people should want to follow.

Leadership is persuasion: Persuasion from the outside ignites motivation from the inside.

Leadership is creativity: The leader sees 'outside the box'. He sees new opportunities. He's not satisfied with the status quo. He creates new visions and new ways to achieve them.

Leadership is self-management: The leader disciplines his own life to be able to fulfil his vision, and he leads his followers to do the same with their lives.

Leadership is character or integrity: Christian leadership is based upon integrity so the "where" and the "how" of the move will be appropriate.

Leadership is credibility: People will only follow someone they believe in.

Leadership is trust: Trust is integral to credibility.

Leadership is modelling: Effective leaders do not merely "say"; they also "do" and thereby show others the way.

Leadership is servanthood: Christian leaders should follow the example of Jesus. This is how the leader helps people move. Servanthood pervades good leadership. The heart of a true leader is to help his people become all they can be in God. The essence of servant leadership is seeking what is best for the followers in the purposes of God, and not of oneself.

2. THERE ARE THREE ESSENTIAL PARTS TO THIS LEADERSHIP DEFINITION:

The leader establishes the direction. He aligns the people in that direction. He motivates and inspires them to move in that direction, and to fulfil the vision.

2.1. THE LEADER ESTABLISHES THE DIRECTION

This is one of the primary roles of leadership. Good leaders are pioneers. They continually search for new opportunities to do what has never been done before. They are not content to merely maintain the status quo. Moreover, leaders see the great potential in their *followers* (constituents) and want them to fulfil it. To do this effectively, the leader must be able to perceive not only the opportunities that are before the organization, but also the obstacles that stand in the way. Failure to do so will result in failed ventures and follies that discredit the leader and discourage his followers. Thus, leadership is more than just grandiose 'visionary' talk; anyone can talk big, like the story of the boy who cried 'wolf.' After a while, no one believed him anymore. So it is with many leaders who continually 'cry vision' when it is not realistic. After a while, no one believes them anymore. Good leaders have a vision that is realistic.

2.2. THE LEADER ALIGNS THE PEOPLE IN THAT DIRECTION

After perceiving the opportunities, the leader must then translate them into organisational goals and enlist the people in the achievement of those goals. The people must clearly understand and personally own the vision. This takes time. Leaders who have spent months or even years developing their vision should not expect the people to jump on board the first time they hear it. People need time to understand it and to wrestle with its cost. In addition, the people are usually not as oriented to action and change as the leader is.

For any change there will be both risk and a price that needs to be paid. The people must count the cost and be willing to move.

A common error of visionary leaders is that they attempt to jump from establishing the direction to beginning the move toward its achievement. Visionary leaders must be patient with their people! They must effectively align the people first.

The primary instrument of alignment is communication. To be effective, communication must be clear, passionate and credible.

In this process of alignment, the leader must realistically assess his followers' needs and abilities. Moreover, he must ensure that the vision is personally meaningful enough to his people to gain their commitment and effort.

As we will see, one primary difference between a good leader and a bad one is this:

> A good leader's vision serves the people.

> A bad leader's vision serves the leader himself.

2.3. THE LEADER MOTIVATES AND INSPIRES THE PEOPLE TO IMPLEMENT AND ACHIEVE THE VISION

Once the people genuinely share the vision, they must be led in its implementation and fulfilment. This requires role modelling on the part of the leader (Heb. 13:7). He must demonstrate his total dedication to the cause he shares with his followers – even to the point of accepting personal risk and making self-sacrifice for the good of the organization (Phil. 1:29-30). He must also empower the people by giving them genuine responsibility as well as the authority to fulfil that responsibility. Finally, the leader must continually encourage them to keep moving in the right direction (Phil. 1:6; Gal. 6:9).

3. JESUS FULFILMENT OF THREE PARTS OF LEADERSHIP

The three parts of leadership in Jesus' Great Commission:

> Then Jesus came to them and said, "all authority in heaven and on earth has been given to me. Therefore, go and make disciples of all nations, baptizing them in the name of the Father and of the Son and of the Holy Spirit, and teaching them to obey everything I have commanded you. And surely, I am with you always, to the very end of the age." (Matt. 28:18-20)

Jesus established the direction. He shared a clear and compelling vision with His disciples:

> "Make disciples of all nation teaching them to obey everything I have commanded you".

Jesus had already aligned his followers in that direction through what he had already taught them: "everything I have commanded you."

Now he aligned them in the specific direction he wanted them to go and said, "Start moving...":

> "Go and make disciples of all nations, baptizing them in the name of the Father and of the Son and of the Holy Spirit, and teaching them to obey everything I have commanded you."

Finally, Jesus motivated and inspired them to keep moving and to fulfil the vision:

> "Surely, I am with you always, to the very end of the age."

Let's remember this: "A leader helps someone move from where he is now to somewhere else."

3. THE WORLDVIEW ON LEADERSHIP

Christian leadership worldview generally agreed that there is a marked difference between Christian and non-Christian methods of leadership. Yet, when questioned, many believers struggle to explain what these differences are. Christian leaders themselves don't fare much better, a fact which becomes especially evident when we survey much of the so-called Christian leadership literature doing the rounds in evangelical circles today. Oftentimes these are little more than a repeat of conventional secular wisdom, sprinkled with Bible verses to sanctify and legitimise their use.

If there is a difference between secular and Christian leadership styles, then what is it? Furthermore, how big is this difference? Is Christian leadership complimentary to secular leadership, or does it present an alternative to secular leadership? To put it in picture form: Is it the roof rack of the vehicle, or is it another vehicle altogether? (Westhuizen)

The difference between secular and Christian leadership is the very difference separating the Kingdom of God from the fallen empires of this world. It is, in other words, that difference that contrasts light and darkness, life and death. To put the two together as though they are variants of the same species won't do. They stand unalterably antithetical, and so they will remain until the day of the Lord.

We have all heard it said that Hitler was an excellent leader. By this it is usually meant that he had great charisma and even greater powers of conviction. He managed to lead thousands, and so we conclude that he was a great leader. The fact that he led them to destruction is beside the point. It makes him a poor theorist, perhaps, but not a poor leader. He could get people to follow him, and this is the biggest test of leadership. As John Maxwell said: "If no one is following, you are not leading but merely taking a walk." We could turn that around to mean that if people are following, you are definitely leading. (Maxwell 11).

The Christian worldview of leadership is different from most secular worldviews on the subject. In the secular, leadership tends to be viewed primarily in terms of a company's bottom line and how well the leader can urge employees to produce more and better work. That view is profit-centred rather than person-centred, and it does not give much attention to employees' human needs and qualities nor on how developing excellent work relationships can promote productivity. In the Christian worldview, however, people are key, and their human needs are important. The leader in the Christian worldview understands how meeting employees' needs promotes the kind of productivity desired and how developing strong work relationships can do more for the company's success than micromanaging or other forms of harassment can achieve. (Bartle).

Howard Schultz, the CEO of Starbucks, made the following observation:

> "I think it's very difficult to lead today when people are not truly participating in the decision. You won't be able to attract and retain great people if they don't feel like they are part of the authorship of the strategy and the authorship of the critical issues. If you don't give

people an opportunity to really be engaged, they won't stay" (Schultz 41).

In secular leadership, one of the goals you got given as a leader is most likely to attract and keep workers motivated. So, let's explore the five key traits that a secular leader needs to have under his belt to be successful:

Key Trait 1: You must have a vision.

We've all heard the saying "You must stand for something, or you'll fall for everything." But what does that really mean? Standing firm when it comes to your company's policies and procedures is all well and good, but it doesn't speak to having a vision. As a leader, you must learn to communicate your vision or the vision of your company to the people you want to follow you. But how can you do that?

- o Learn to paint a picture with words. Speak it, write it, draw it, touch it. Whatever methods you can use to create a picture, do it. As they say, "A picture is worth a thousand words."

- o Ask each of the other managers in your company to tell you, in their own words, about the vision of the company. How close is it to what you thought they understood? Is your team on the same page as you?

- o As you work, your company's vision should be in your mind every day, and you should re-evaluate it occasionally so that it stays current with the changing times in which we live. And remember, your staff needs to be just as involved as you in keeping it up to date if you truly want them to buy in on the vision. Be sure to keep your key players involved.

Key Trait 2: You must have passion.

Your employees want passion; in fact, they'll go to the ends of earth because of it, live and die for it. Think of the sailors who travelled with Christopher Columbus or Leif Ericsson to explore uncharted territory. Their leaders' passion inspired them to take on new and very dangerous challenges.

To build an extraordinary management team, you've got to light the 'fire in their bellies', to get them to feel passion about the company and connect to the leader's vision. Passion is such a key part of being a great leader that if you don't have it, you simply can't be a great leader. Think of all the great leaders throughout the ages and try to name one that did not have passion.

Passion is infectious: When you talk about your vision for the company, let your passion for your vision shine through. Others will feel it and want to get on board with you. If you don't have passion for your vision, you need to recreate your vision or reframe your description of your vision, so it's connected to your passion.

Key Trait 3: You must learn to be a great decision maker.

How are major decisions made in your company? What is your process for making them? For instance, do you talk to your management team and create a list of pros and cons to help you make the best decision? Maybe you conduct a cost analysis. Or do you create a timeline for the implementation strategy, process and timing?

Some leaders have a set process, and others fly by the seat of their pants. You don't want to be one of those leaders who consults no one before deciding on and announcing the change the next day and then gets frustrated when no one follows it. If you're one of those leaders, it's time to implement a set process.

In fact, here's a system a leader can use to become a better decision maker. It's called the Q-CAT:

- Q = Quick. Be quick but not hasty.
- C = Committed. Be committed to your decision but not rigid.
- A = Analytical. Be analytical, but don't over analyse as too much analysis can cause decision paralysis.
- T = Thoughtful. Be thoughtful about all concerned, but don't be obsessive.

When you use the Q-CAT, it'll help you to decide when to bring others into the process and what steps need to be taken to help you make better decisions.

Key Trait 4: You must be a team builder.

To become a great leader, you must develop a great team or, one might say, a well-oiled machine. But how do you do that? You can start by handing off responsibility to your team and letting your team to run with it. Don't breathe down their necks, and don't micromanage, but make yourself available if questions or problems come up. Teach your team to use the Q-CAT decision-making system and give them the freedom to work through their own decisions.

When projects aren't on track or your team is falling behind on deadline, it serves no one if you start pointing fingers. This is when you need to rise to the occasion and inspire confidence in your employees, to let them know you support them and are ready to help. Be ready to alter plans and make new ones. Don't forget to use humour to keep your team's spirits up during a crisis. When an emergency hits, your team will look to you to be a tower of strength and endurance.

Key Trait 5: You must have character.

Without character, all the other 'keys' are for naught. That's because your innate character strengths and limitations play a critical role in your leadership style. The real question is, are you aware of just what role they play? All great leaders have taken steps to learn about their individual personality and what part it plays in their leadership style. It's a good way to do a "character check" on yourself and your leadership skills.

Then, once you've done the assessment, the question to ask yourself is: do you feel your character matches what the assessments are pointing out to you? If you feel the traits don't match who you think you are, then look a little deeper and be honest with yourself. Sometimes our first response is defensive. You might want to assess yourself with a different type of profile and then compare the results. Within the 360 Degree Feedback model, there's an opportunity to see how your employees and peers view you, too. In learning to be a great leader, the first step is to be open to feedback about yourself as a leader and separate it from you as the person (Maxwell 189).

According to leadership worldview to be great leader is to be someone who has a clear vision and can turn that vision into a vivid picture that others can see. When you speak about your vision, it should be with a passion you feel in your heart, a passion that creates so much enthusiasm that your team will want to jump on board. When major decisions need to be made, you should encourage everyone to use the Q-CAT system and be responsible for his or her own actions. You should be continually assessing your own character and never stop growing, personally or professionally.

If you can apply the five keys to great leadership, you'll be well on your way to becoming a great leader surrounded by great employees.

In the secular approach to leadership, there is an inherent belief that hard work will get you to the top and guarantee success.

Max DePree, the retired Chairman of Herman Miller says, "The first responsibility of a leader is to define reality." How a leader defines reality is contingent on the lenses through which he sees reality: his perspective. Philosophers and anthropologists talk about a worldview as a way of seeing on the world, a perspective of things, a way of looking at the cosmos from a particular vantage point (DePree).

In philosophy, a worldview is perceived mainly in cognitive dimensions, leaving out the affective and moral scopes. Anthropologists cast worldview as culture which is "an integrated coherent way of mentally organising the world" and includes the more personal aspects of interpretation. These mental grids are the basis for a leader's decisions and behaviours.

Perspectives provide context to frame events so that meaningful interpretations can emerge to inform decisions or responses. They also shape assumptions and presuppositions that guide our reasoning and conclusions.

The most intimate context that influences a leader is his self-perception. This is the 'Being' lens that will inform his decisions and direction. Three important 'Being' questions shape a leader's perspectives.

'Who Am I?' reflects on the identity of the leader. The answers to the question will disclose if the leader has assumed responsibility for how he has turned out in life. They will determine how he relates to others; if he readily initiates solutions, or blames others when things go wrong; whether the leader will be secure enough to empower or honour co-workers and subordinates; and whether the leader can be himself without pretensions.

These are contingent on his answers to this question. To be true to oneself will bring fulfilment, making a leader's honest answers to this critical question a predictor of his contentment quotient. The response to this foundational question will raise the ultimate concern to the leader: 'What is most important to me?' To win at all costs may be the stance of some leaders arising from who they are while the perspective of others may demonstrate a 'win-win', 'share-the-benefits' disposition.

The second question, 'Where Am I?' reveals the leader's understanding of process and posture. It shapes the leader's consciousness of his role and the limitation of his time in the position of influence and responsibility. It helps to define the leader's contribution in the context of past achievements and future challenges. This question invites the leader to understand and appreciate contributions of past leaders in the organisation, so the incumbent can build on past achievements and recognise the shoulders on which he stands. It allows the leader to interpret successes and challenges from both a short term and long-term perspective. It also instils hope in the possibilities of improvement, recognising that where we are now does not necessarily define where we will be tomorrow. It encourages the attitude of life-long learning.

When a leader is conscious that he will not be in office permanently, he will understand his responsibility and the necessity to nurture younger leaders. He realises he will not be where he is now perpetually. Perhaps the most toxic characteristic of strong leaders is their reluctance to vacate their position or office. Whether in nations, commerce or church, the legacy of a strong leader's intent on staying in office for life is the death of what they have sought to build. When leaders are oblivious to the transitory nature of their tenure, they expend energy in preserving their power rather than building values and nurturing emerging leaders. Understanding 'where I am' not only helps a leader seize present opportunities but also build a stronger future.

The final query, 'Whose Am I?' plumbs the emotive and affective depths of the leader. It explores the elusive domain of meaning, reaching for an answer to Who am I working for?', 'Why am I doing for what I am doing?' These questions help leaders understand the importance and place of significant relationships; that people are not minions or inconvenient extensions of arms needed to perform work or means of profit.

Without the relational dimension, personal success may end up empty. The question also provides perspective when relational conflicts and intractable people-situations require forgiveness, generosity, and the possibility of second chances. It is in the relational dimension that meaning and purpose in life can be found, that hope in finding a way out of intractable situations can be discovered.

The implications for leadership behaviour are significant when a leader understands he belongs to God, who has loved him in Jesus Christ. Philosopher Geddes MacGregor points to God's infinite power that springs from creative love: "That is, the power that is infinite, being infinitely creative and therefore infinitely sacrificial. God does not control his creatures; He graciously lets them be, divine almightiness consists, not in God's possession of an unlimited ability to do what he pleases, but of unlimited capacity for creative love, so that not only does he bring creatures into being to let them be but he creatively restores whatever seeks such restoration, so that the redeemed might indeed well be called a new creation, that is, a re-creation. God has no ambitions to fulfil our goals to attain for his aggrandisement. The only way he could go in his creative act would be a way of self-limitation, self-emptying, self-abnegation." (Chao)

The leader who is embraced by God's love is self-giving rather than self-serving and he is redemptive rather than dismissive. The leader has power and authority, but not to destroy an underperforming employee's future or manipulate people to fulfil his ambitions. Instead, he seeks to redeem mistakes and create opportunities for subordinates to find their 'sweet spot' so they may succeed and flourish. Only a secure leader can be self-giving and not be suspicious and self-protective. Only one who knows who he is can be secure. As MacGregor concludes, "self-sacrificial love would then be an inalienable character of being."

It is in the *Being* of the leader that core values reside. These values are convictions that hold the leader to responsible, predictable behaviour and decisions.

In the secular world, courage is one of the ingredients that a leader must have, that is also true in Christian worldview, but the difference is that, in Christian leadership, the courage is not from a leader's personal ability but because he trusts in the Lord instead of relying on self courage.

Courage has its root in the French word **Cœur**, meaning 'heart'. It remains a common metaphor for inner strength, frequently used broadly for "what is in one's mind or thoughts." Courageous leaders find resolve to determine action in a crisis and take a position in a debate. Otherwise, there is no moving forward and confusion will demoralise the people in the organisation. To Winston Churchill, "courage is rightly esteemed the first of human qualities…because it is the quality which guarantees all others."

In biblical perspective, it is apparent that courage is an indispensable leadership virtue. Leading in crises or momentous times can be disheartening and discouraging. These are occasions when it seems the cause is lost and the future bleak. Many are quick to give opinions, but few are willing to assume responsibility for leading change. People walk out when their own interests cannot be fulfilled, but true leaders find the courage to stay and make changes so that others can be blessed.

Leaders need to demonstrate courage most at these two critical points of decisions:

3.1 DIRECTION FOR THE FUTURE

In both success and crisis, leaders need to take their organisations into the future. There are always conflicting evidence and dissenting voices seeking to influence decisions on future direction. There can be different interpretations of the same data, motivated by vested interests. In a season of dazzling success, the temptation is to repeat or expand the formula that resulted in triumph and fill the future with more of the same. When organisations are challenged in vision and resources, they are most inclined to look over the fence and be seduced into replicating others' successful models. It's all about mechanics and methodology in searching out a winning formula, never mind if there a cultural or vocational fit. This is where leaders are tempted to exchange form for substance, and end route to the future, risk a hollowing out of the organisation, losing its vision and reason for being.

Leaders need the courage to remain faithful to their vision, which is the rudder that determines the direction to go from hence. Bill Hybels defines vision as "a picture of the future that produces passion" (Hybels). It entails two components. Firstly, the calling of the leader in response to specific needs, and secondly, the energizing compulsion in the leader's being towards fulfilling that call. If the calling came from God, the fire of passion in the leader's heart will not wane. To the contrary, the leader is infectiously excited by the vision and inspires and mobilises others to join him in realising the vision. Gregg Thompson, the President of Bluepoint Leadership Development says that "great leaders know that there cannot be genuine power without courage – the courage to act" (Thompson).

William Wilberforce took on the cause of the abolition of slavery in 1787 and kept true to that vision through the repeated failures in the British Parliament until it prevailed in 1833 with the Slavery Abolition Act, just before he died. Nelson Mandela was imprisoned for 27 years while he held tight to the vision of anti-apartheid and acted on that vision till his cause ended in victory. The vision and the call prescribed the path to the future. It requires courage to discern and declare that vision, and to follow that vision into the future, ignoring distractions and overcoming obstacles.

There is no guarantee that leaders will remain effective and courageous. Max DePree reveals that he has learnt "leaders are fragile precisely at the point of their strengths, liable to fail at the height of their success. A leader's ability to be faithful, especially in relation to the vision and strategy of the institution, is a perpetually open question." Maybe that is why Scriptures constantly remind leaders to "be strong and courageous."

3.2 DISCERNMENT OF PEOPLE

Leaders work with people. Where there are no people, there are no leaders. Perhaps the most critical decisions leaders make are concerning people. A leader once observed, "we hire for competence, but we fire for relational reasons." (Chao) That was a most profound observation that has proven true in almost every recruitment and release of staff in organisations. We look for competencies in the people we hire so they can perform. But social dislocations cause discontent and disgruntlement. Even an incompetent worker is fired only when his co-workers express frustration with his slack performance. The non-performer is already expelled by the community in the organisation before his employment is terminated.

Effective leaders understand that their "fundamental purpose, the reason for being, is to enlarge the lives of others." It takes a lot of courage to make a decision regardless of their performance criteria and the bottom line is always seek to provide meaning to life, not just to look for what it means to make a living. Max DePree asks, "What is it most of us really want from work? ... We would like a work process and relationships that meet our personal needs for belonging, for contributing, for meaningful work, for the opportunity to make a commitment, for the opportunity to grow and be at least reasonably in control of our own destinies."

Leaders must realise that people will not contribute fully until they get what they need from their leaders. When leaders find the courage to care for their followers they build trust, which inspires people to give their best to fulfil corporate goals.

The other view of leadership is about the way you perceive and treat yourself, and how you perceive and treat others. Personal leadership involves the former; social and organisational leadership involves the latter. The two are interrelated.

Every leader has a unique, complex way of thinking, which he has developed since birth. This complex system is believed to be a composite of several more fundamental thinking systems layered one on top of the other. Our worldview is the totality of our conception of what this complex, fragmented world is like. Our worldview is a composite of our cognitive style, genetic makeup, memory, mental models or paradigms, assumptions, vision of the future, and the fusion of factual and value premises. Our personal worldview plays a major role in determining outcomes in our personal lives.

Our collective worldview plays a major role in determining outcomes in our organisations and institutions. This is often described as the "See-Do-Get" cycle. How we "see the world" determines "what we do," and "what we do" determines "what we get" as an outcome (Baker 26).

Dr. Stephen Covey states that all things are created twice. There is a "first creation," which is of the mind, and a "second creation," which is the physical manifestation of the first creation. For instance, a blueprint is the first creation, and the building is the second creation. Our attitudes and behaviours flow from our worldview (Covey 17).

Each one of us filters the information we receive about the world through our worldview to determine what we consider truth. Our personal worldview will change and become more complex as we grow older and mature. Collective worldviews can follow the same pattern of maturation. Albert Einstein understood this when he observed, "the significant problems we face cannot be solved at the same level of thinking we were at when we created them."

Our worldview is our mind's way of dealing with what Dr. Michael Armour calls the "Four Big C's": Change, Complexity, Confusion, and Conflict. As we grow older, and our worldview can no longer sufficiently cope with the four C's, we may experience a paradigm shift to a higher system of thinking. The mind activates more complex systems of thinking to cope with new problems. Rather than totally replacing our old worldview with a new one, we integrate parts of our old worldview with the new (Armour).

The perception you have of yourself is part of your worldview. It involves such issues as your personal accountability, values that matter most to you, your personal mission in life, and the importance of self-discipline. It also defines what you must do to hedge against leading an inconsequential life.

The answer to important life issues will depend on your maturity level. It is generally recognised that lower levels of maturity exhibit extremely self-serving worldviews. The worldview of an infant, for example, is totally self-centred. The result of an infant's worldview is a life consisting of a series of short-term reactions to physiological needs such as nourishment, warmth, and so on. As the maturity of an individual increases, there is a shift from reactivity to proactivity. Proactivity means that our behaviour is a function of our decisions, not our conditions. Higher levels of maturity demonstrate consideration for others and self-sacrifice.

Many leaders stop reconstructing their worldview at different maturity levels, thus creating the incredible diversity of thought we see in our world today. We must understand that there are different worldviews. Each one of us has a unique worldview. However, there are similar worldview patterns that result in similar pursuits and standards of conduct.

Since our worldview determines how we lead others and ourselves, there is also a great deal of diversity of thought regarding leadership. Leadership models can be viewed along a continuum. At one end of the continuum, we can find the power model, with its authoritarian style. At this end of the continuum, we find a top-down, command-and-control pyramid approach, with powerful decision-makers at the top. At the other end of the continuum is where we find servant leadership and similar leadership models. At this end of the continuum, we find a worldview that sees the world as an interdependent reality where people are treated with respect in a totally egalitarian manner.

The purpose of the mission often determines the use of a given model. For instance, an authoritarian command and control model of leadership may be very effective for stopping something, destroying something, or conquering something, such as an enemy during a war. The military has used the power leadership model for millennia very effectively. It is a leadership model that is hard-nosed and aggressive in style. The power model of leadership often involves the formation of privileged classes, strict hierarchy, turf protection, intimidation, and rank. Unfortunately, one can find many examples of the inappropriate use of this model of leadership today in corporations, government agencies, and churches. It is interesting to note that modern military organisations use a variety of leadership models to deal with the numerous complex roles they play in our modern world. (Johannsen)

If the objective or mission is to build an organisation dedicated to service such as public service, customer service, or serving a congregation, empowerment, creativity, and the growth and maturing of individuals, then the power model of leadership is highly inappropriate. A leadership model based on a totally different system of thinking should be considered.

Our worldview determines our belief regarding whether the power model or servant leadership model is ever a legitimate approach. Our worldview also determines when we think it would be appropriate for us to use either model of leadership. Unfortunately, some worldviews see only one model as appropriate for all situations. As Abraham Maslow said, "He that is good with a hammer tends to think everything is a nail." (Maslow) Other worldviews acknowledge the servant leadership model as legitimate but attempt to implement it using authoritarian and patriarchal methods. Addressing this problem, Peter Block states, "the very system that has patriarchy as the root problem uses patriarchal means to try to eliminate its symptoms. This is the dark side of leadership" (Block).

In secular worldview we have a lot of leadership model and theories.

3.3 THE SITUATIONAL LEADERSHIP MODEL

This model of leadership is arguably the most recognised, utilised and effective leadership and influence tool in the history of the behaviour sciences.

This approach sees leadership as specific to the situation in which it is being exercised. For example, whilst some situations may require an autocratic style, others may need a more participative approach. It also proposes that there may be differences in required leadership styles at different levels in the same organisation.

Developed by Dr. Paul Hersey in the late 1960s, the Situational Leadership Model is a powerful, yet flexible tool that enables leaders of all kinds; managers, salespeople, peer leaders, teachers or parents to more effectively influence others.

The situational leadership theory, developed by Paul Hersey and Ken Blanchard (1977), is based upon two continuums: the required level of supervision and arousal required to coach workers in specific situations so that they develop into great performers:

- Supervision (directing) - The employee's skill and knowledge level determines the level of supervision, what Hershey and Blanchard call Directing. On one end of the continuum is over-supervision, while on the other end is under-supervision. The goal is to hit the sweet spot. Under-supervision leads to miscommunication, lack of coordination, and the perception by subordinates that the leader does not care. Over-supervision stifles initiative, breeds resentment, and lowers morale. The goal is to provide the correct amount of supervision that is determined by the employee's skill and knowledge level.

- Arousal (supporting) - The employee's skill and knowledge level determines the amount of arousal or emotional support required what the authors call Supporting. This emotional support raises or lowers the task holder's arousal level (the inner drive within our self-system). A certain level of arousal motivates us toward change (learning). However, too much or too little will over or under stimulate our behaviour. In highly cognitive tasks a low arousal is required as over-simulation may occur and vice-versa.

Blanchard (1985) later refined the model and changed the term Situational Leadership Theory to simply Situational Leadership. In his model, leadership is the act of providing the correct amount of supervision Directing Behaviour and arousal Supportive Behaviour, which can in return, produce the best learning and developmental environment as shown in the model below (Blanchard).

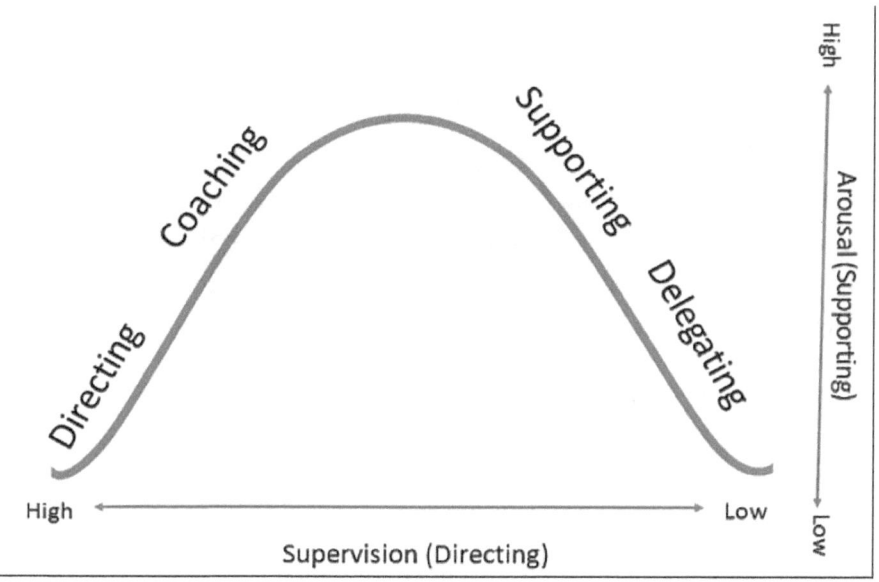

Situational Leadership is basically a four-step model, or four leadership styles described in it, however, depending upon the situation, you can jump into any step or leadership style as required depending on how well an employee can perform and is motivated to perform. Let's try to grasp the meaning of these following words, which we will better define later.

> Directing - Provide a lot of direction; learner does not know how to perform and a small amount of support, you do not want to overload learner.
>
> Coaching - Decrease direction so that learner can learn by trial and error and increase support needs emotional support due to some failure.
>
> Supporting - Decrease direction even more so that the learner can become self-supporting and decrease support.

Delegating - Provide direction and support on an as-needed basis.

3.4 REVIEW OF LEADERSHIP THEORY

A review of the leadership literature reveals an evolving series of schools of thought from 'Great Man' and 'Trait' theories to 'Transformational' leadership. Whilst early theories tend to focus upon the characteristics and behaviours of successful leaders, later theories begin to consider the role of followers and the contextual nature of leadership (Bolden., Gosling, Marturano, Dennison).

a. GREAT MAN THEORIES

Based on the belief that leaders are exceptional people, born with innate qualities, destined to lead. The use of the term 'man' was intentional since until the latter part of the twentieth century leadership was thought of as a concept which is primarily male, military and Western. This led to the next school of Trait Theories.

b. TRAIT THEORIES

The lists of traits or qualities associated with leadership exist in abundance and continue to be produced. They draw on virtually all the adjectives in the dictionary which describe some positive or virtuous human attribute, from ambition to zest for life.

c. BEHAVIOURIST THEORIES

These concentrate on what leaders do rather than on their qualities. Different patterns of behaviour are observed and categorised as 'styles of leadership'. This area has probably attracted most attention on practising managers.

d. CONTINGENCY THEORY

This is a refinement of the situational viewpoint and focuses on identifying the situational variables which best predict the most appropriate or effective leadership style to fit particular circumstances.

e. TRANSACTIONAL THEORY

This approach emphasises the importance of the relationship between leader and followers, focusing on the mutual benefits derived from some kind of contract through which the leader delivers such things as rewards or recognition in return for the commitment or loyalty of the followers.

f. TRANSFORMATIONAL THEORY

The central concept here is change and the role of leadership in envisioning and implementing the transformation of organisational performance from 'Great Man' to 'Transformational' Leadership.

Each of these theories takes a rather individualistic perspective of the leader, although a school of thought gaining increasing recognition is that of 'dispersed' leadership. This approach, with its foundations in sociology, psychology and politics rather than management science, views leadership as a process that is diffuse throughout an organisation rather than lying solely with the formally designated 'leader'. The emphasis thus shifts from developing 'leaders' to developing 'leaderful' organisations with a collective responsibility for leadership. (De Bono, Remme, Jones, Heijden).

In the current section we will focus primarily on the more traditional, individualistic views of the leader as we feel these have greatest relevance to the development of management and leadership standards.

The Trait Approach to Leadership arose from the "Great Man" theory as a way of identifying the key characteristics of successful leaders. It was believed that through this approach critical leadership traits could be isolated and that people with such traits could then be recruited, selected, and installed into leadership positions. This approach was common in the military and is still used as a set of criteria to select candidates for commissions.

The problem with the trait approach lies in the fact that almost as many traits as studies undertaken were identified. After several years of such research, it became apparent that no consistent traits could be identified. Although some traits were found in a considerable number of studies, the results were generally inconclusive. Some leaders might have possessed certain traits but the absence of them did not necessarily mean that the person was not a leader.

Although there was little consistency in the results of the various trait studies, some traits did appear more frequently than others, including: technical skill, friendliness, task motivation, application to task, group task supportiveness, social skill, emotional control, administrative skill, general charisma, and intelligence. Of these, the most widely explored has tended to be charisma.

Stogdill identified a list of the main leadership traits and skills (Stogdill 28).

Traits:
- Adaptable to situations
- Alert to social environment
- Ambitious and achievement-orientated
- Assertive
- Cooperative
- Decisive
- Dependable
- Dominant (desire to influence others)
- Energetic (high activity level)
- Persistent

- Self-confident
- Tolerant of stress
- Willing to assume responsibility.

Skills:
- Clever (intelligent)
- Conceptually skilled
- Creative
- Diplomatic and tactful
- Fluent in speaking
- Knowledgeable about group task
- Organised (administrative ability)
- Persuasive
- Socially skilled

At the Behavioural School the results of the trait studies were inconclusive. Traits, amongst other things, were hard to measure. How, for example, do we measure traits such as honesty, integrity, loyalty, or diligence? Another approach in the study of leadership had to be found.

After the publication of the late Douglas McGregor's classic book The Human Side of Enterprise in 1960, attention shifted to "behavioural theories." McGregor was a teacher, researcher, and consultant whose work was considered as being "on the cutting edge" of managing people. He influenced all the behavioural theories, which emphasise focusing on human relationships, along with output and performance. (McGregor 22).

McGregor's Theory X & Theory Y Managers Although not strictly speaking a theory of leadership, the leadership strategy of effectively used participative management proposed in Douglas McGregor's book has had a tremendous impact on managers. The most publicised concept is McGregor's thesis that leadership strategies are influenced by a leader's assumptions about human nature. As a result of his experience as a consultant, McGregor summarised two contrasting sets of assumptions made by managers in industry.

Theory X managers believe that:

The average human being has an inherent dislike of work and will avoid it if possible. Because of this human characteristic, most people must be coerced, controlled, directed, or threatened with punishment to get them to put forth adequate effort to achieve organisational objectives.

The average human being prefers to be directed, wishes to avoid responsibility, has relatively little ambition, and wants security above all else.

Theory Y managers believe that:

The expenditure of physical and mental effort in work is as natural as play or rest, and the average human being, under proper conditions, learns not only to accept but to seek responsibility.

People will exercise self-direction and self-control to achieve objectives to which they are committed.

The capacity to exercise a relatively high level of imagination, ingenuity, and creativity in the solution of organisational problems is widely, not narrowly, distributed in the population, and the intellectual potential of the average human being is only partially utilised under the conditions of modern industrial life.

The Blake Mouton Managerial Grid (Blake & Mouton, 1964) proposes that team management, a high concern for both employees and production, is the most effective type of leadership behaviour.

The Contingency or Situational School

Whilst behavioural theories may help managers develop particular leadership behaviours, they give little guidance as to what constitutes effective leadership in different situations. Indeed, most researchers today conclude that no one leadership style is right for every manager. Instead, contingency-situational theories were developed to indicate that the style to be used is contingent upon such factors as the situation, the people, the task, the organisation, and other environmental variables. The major theories contributing towards this school of thought are described below (Fiedler).

Fiedler's Contingency Model postulates that there is no single best way for managers to lead. Situations will create different leadership style requirements for a manager. The solution to a managerial situation is contingent on the factors that impinge on the situation. For example, in a highly routine (mechanistic) environment where repetitive tasks are the norm, a relatively directive leadership style may result in the best performance. In a dynamic environment a more flexible, participative style may be required.

Fiedler looked at three situations that could define the condition of a managerial task:

a. Leader member relations: How well do the manager and the employees get along?

b. Task structure: Is the job highly structured, fairly unstructured, or somewhere in between?

c. Position power: How much authority does the manager possess?

Managers were rated as to whether they were relationship oriented or task oriented. Task oriented managers tend to do better in situations that have good leader-member relationships, structured tasks, and either weak or strong position power.

They do well when the task is unstructured, but position power is strong. They also do well at the other end of the spectrum, when the leader-member relations were moderate to poor, and the task was unstructured.

Relationship oriented managers do better in all other situations. Thus, a given situation might call for a manager with a different style or a manager who could take on a different style for a different situation.

These environmental variables are combined in a weighted sum that is favourable at one end and unfavourable at the other. Task oriented style is preferable at the clearly defined extremes of favourable and unfavourable environments, but relationship orientation excels in the middle ground. Leaders could attempt to reshape the environment variables to match their style.

Another aspect of the contingency model theory is that the leader-member relations, task structure, and position power dictate a leader's situational control. Leader-member relations are the amount of loyalty, dependability, and support that the leader receives from employees. It is a measure of how the manager perceives he or she and the group of employees is getting along. In a favourable relationship the manager has a high task structure and can reward and/or punish employees without any problems. In an unfavourable relationship the task is usually unstructured, and the leader possesses limited authority. The spelling out in detail favourable of what is required of subordinates affects task structure.

Positioning power measures the amount of power or authority the manager perceives the organisation has given him or her for the purpose of directing, rewarding, and punishing subordinates. Positioning power of managers depends on taking away favourable or increasing unfavourable the decision-making power of employees.

The task-motivated style leader experiences pride and satisfaction in the task accomplishment for the organisation, while the relationship-motivated style seeks to build interpersonal relations and extend extra help for the team development in the organisation. There is no good or bad leadership style. Each person has his or her own preferences for leadership. Task-motivated leaders are at their best when the group performs successfully such as achieving a new sales record or outperforming the major competitor. Relationship-oriented leaders are at their best when greater customer satisfaction is gained, and a positive company image is established.

The Hersey-Blanchard Model of Leadership also takes a situational perspective of leadership. (Blanchard). This model posits that the developmental levels of a leader's subordinates play the greatest role in determining which leadership styles leader behaviours are most appropriate. Their theory is based on the amount of direction, task behaviour, socio-emotional support, and relationship behaviour a leader must provide given the situation and the level of maturity of the followers.

Task behaviour is the extent to which the leader engages in spelling out the duties and responsibilities to an individual or group. This behaviour includes telling people what to do, how to do it, when to do it, where to do it, and who is to do it. In task behaviour the leader engages in one-way communication.

Relationship behaviour is the extent to which the leader engages in two-way or multi-way communications. This includes listening, facilitating, and supportive behaviours. In relationship behaviour the leader engages in two-way communication by providing socio-emotional support.

Maturity is the willingness and ability of a person to take responsibility for directing his or her own behaviour. People tend to have varying degrees of maturity, depending on the specific task, function, or objective that a leader is attempting to accomplish through their efforts.

In summary therefore, leader behaviours fall along two continua:

Directive behaviour and supportive behaviour involve one-way communication. In directive behaviour, followers' roles are clearly communicated and there is close supervision of performance. For supportive behaviour there is a two-way communication; listening, providing support and encouragement, and facilitating interaction for follower in decision-making.

As we said earlier in the book, for Blanchard the key situational variable when determining the appropriate leadership style, is the readiness or developmental level of the subordinates. As a result, four leadership styles are suggested:

a. Directing: The leader provides clear instructions and specific direction. This style is best matched with a low follower readiness level.

b. Coaching: The leader encourages two-way communication and helps build confidence and motivation on the part of the employee, although the leader still has responsibility and controls decision making. Selling style is best matched with a moderate follower readiness level.

c. Supporting: With this style, the leader and followers share decision making and no longer need or expect the relationship to be directive. Participating style is best matched with a moderate follower readiness level.

d. Delegating: This style is appropriate for leaders whose followers are ready to accomplish a particular task and are both competent and motivated to take full responsibility. Delegating style is best matched with a high follower readiness level.

To determine the appropriate leadership style to use in each situation, the leader must first determine the maturity level of the followers in relation to the specific task that the leader is attempting to accomplish through the effort of the followers. As the level of followers' maturity increases, the leader should begin to reduce his or her task behaviour and increase relationship behaviour until the followers reach a moderate level of maturity. As the followers begin to move into an above average level of maturity, the leader should decrease not only task behaviour but also relationship behaviour. Once the maturity level is identified, the appropriate leadership style can be determined.

Tannenbaum & Schmidt's Leadership Continuum One criticism of early work on leadership styles is that they looked at styles in black and white terms. The autocratic and democratic styles, or task-oriented and relationship-oriented styles, which they described are extreme, whereas in practice the behaviour of many, perhaps most, leaders in business will be somewhere between the two. Contingency theorists Tannenbaum and Schmidt suggested that leadership behaviour varies along a continuum and that as one moves away from the autocratic extreme the amount of subordinate participation and involvement in decision taking increases. They also suggested that the kind of leadership represented by the democratic extreme of the continuum will be rarely encountered in formal organisations. (Tannenbaum, Schmidt 33)

Four main leadership styles can be located at points along such a continuum:

- **Autocratic**: The leader takes the decisions and announces them, expecting subordinates to carry them out without question; **the telling style**.

- **Persuasive**: At this point the leader also takes all the decisions for the group without discussion or consultation but believes that people will be better motivated if they are persuaded that the decisions are good ones. He or she does a lot of explaining and 'selling' in order to overcome any possible resistance to what he or she wants to do. The leader also puts a lot of energy into creating enthusiasm for the goals he or she has set for the group; **the selling style.**

- **Consultative**: In this style the leader confers with the group members before making decisions and, in fact, considers their advice and their feelings when framing these decisions. He or she may not always accept the subordinates' advice, but they are likely to feel that they can have some influence. Under this leadership style the decision and the full responsibility for it remain with the leader but the degree of involvement by subordinates in decision taking is very much greater than telling or selling styles: **the consulting style.**

- **Democratic**: Using this style the leader would characteristically lay the problem before his or her subordinates and invite discussion. The leader's role is that of conference leader, or chair, rather than that of decision taker. He or she will allow the decision to emerge out of the process of group discussion, instead of imposing it on the group as its boss: **the joining style.**

What distinguishes this approach from previous discussions of leadership style is that there will be some situations in which each of the above styles is likely to be more appropriate than the others.

- **Telling**: In an emergency, a telling style may be most appropriate and would normally be considered justified by the group if the general climate of that group is supportive and mature.

- **Selling**: The selling style would tend to fit situations in which the group leader, and he or she alone, possesses all the information on which the decision must be based and calls for a very high level of commitment and enthusiasm on the part of group members if the task is to be carried through successfully.

- **Consulting**: The consulting style is likely to be most appropriate when there is time during which to reach a considered decision and when the information on which the decision needs to be based lies among the members of the group.

- **Joining**: The joining style is appropriate under similar conditions, with the important exception that this is likely to be appropriate only in those instances where the nature of the responsibility associated with the decision is such that group members are willing to share it with their leader. Alternatively, the leader may be willing to accept responsibility for decisions which he or she has not made personally.

3.5 SITUATIONAL LEADERSHIP

Situational leadership stresses flexibility and simplicity in execution. This theory can equip leaders in the organisation with the tools necessary to skilfully navigate the demands of an increasingly diverse workforce and evolving global marketplace. Infinitely adaptable to any circumstance, the model prepares leaders to address the most pressing challenges pervasive in today's work environment (Hersey, Blanchard, Natemeyer).

a. THE BENEFITS OF SITUATIONAL LEADERSHIP

The Situational Leadership Model uses a repetitive process that the leaders can leverage to effectively influence the behaviour of others.

The process is simple to both understand and apply that its creator, Dr. Paul Hersey, often described it as "organised common sense." At its core, Situational Leadership provides leaders with an understanding of the relationship between an effective style of leadership and the level of readiness that followers exhibit for a specific task. But it does much more than that with application across organisational leaders, first-line managers, individual contributors, and even teams. Situational Leadership utilises task specificity to serve as a mechanism through which leaders maximise their influence-related impact. We call these individuals 'situational leaders' and would contend that they are critical to the success of any organisation.
More specifically, situational leaders:

- Maintain an acute awareness of their innate leadership-related strengths and areas for development. This includes critical skill sets in working in high-performing organisations.

- Conduct highly effective coaching conversations by understanding when a particular leadership style has a high probability of success and when it does not.

- Skilfully influence up, down and across the organisation by knowing when to be consistent and when to be flexible.

- Create more productive teams/organisations by accelerating the development of individuals that are new to their role or task.

- Develop engaged, committed employees by effectively recognising and proactively addressing the dynamics of performance regression.

- Effectively drive behaviour change and business results by communicating through a common, practical language of leadership.

Through the tools associated with the Situational Leadership Model, leaders can approach coaching and influence opportunities through the lens of task-specificity, as opposed to secure notable achievements about a follower's overall level of ability and motivation.

Situational leaders help followers grow and develop by using high-probability leadership styles for each level of performance readiness. This translates to accelerated individual development and the achievement of desired results.

While behaviour change is the chief aim of most adult-learning endeavours, it is not a realistic outcome for standalone, unsupported training events. Focused reinforcement needs to occur in order to ensure learning is retained and long-term behavioural transformation is realised. Notably, next-level manager support is critical. In fact, research suggests an increase of 65% in retention and transfer to on-the-job application when next level managers are actively engaged in the learning process of their direct reports.

Somehow this seems easy; engage managers and the training will produce a desirable result. Clearly, if it were that simple, the challenges associated with training transfer would be non-existent. The fact of the matter is that without a clear process, mutual task alignment and accountability, manager commitment to the pull-through of training remains random, haphazard and difficult to measure.

3.6 THE THREE LEVELS OF LEADERSHIP

This kind of leadership is a model formulated in 2011 by James Scouller (Scouller 34-35). Designed as a practical tool for developing a person's leadership presence, knowhow and skill, it aims to summarise what leaders have to do, not only to bring leadership to their group or organisation, but also to develop themselves technically and psychologically as leaders. It has been classified as an integrated psychological theory of leadership. It is sometimes known as the 3P model of leadership; **P**ublic, **P**rivate and **P**ersonal leadership.

The Three Levels of Leadership model attempts to combine the strengths of older leadership theories (i.e. traits, behavioural/styles, situational, functional) while addressing their limitations and, at the same time, offering a foundation for leaders wanting to apply the philosophies of servant leadership and authentic leadership.

While reviewing the older leadership theories, Scouller highlighted certain limitations in relation to the development of a leader's skill and effectiveness:

> **Trait theory**: As Stogdill (1948) and Buchanan & Huczynski (1997) had previously pointed out, this approach has failed to develop a universally agreed list of leadership qualities and successful leaders seem to defy classification from the trait's perspective. Moreover, because traits theory gave rise to the idea that leaders are born not made, Scouller argued that its approach is better suited to selecting leaders than developing them.
>
> **Behavioural styles theory**: Blake and Mouton, in their managerial grid model, proposed five leadership

styles based on two axes: concern for the task versus concern for people. They suggested that the ideal is the 'team style', which balances concern for the task with concern for people. Scouller argued that this ideal approach may not suit all circumstances, for example, emergencies or turnarounds.

Situational/contingency theories: This includes Hersey & Blanchard's situational leadership theory, House's path–goal theory, Tannenbaum & Schmidt's leadership continuum. Most of these theories assume that leaders can change their behaviour at will to meet differing circumstances, when in practice many find it hard to do so even after training because of unconscious fixed beliefs, fears or ingrained habits. For this reason, leaders need to work on their underlying psychology if they are to attain the flexibility to apply these theories.

Functional theories: Widely used approaches like Kouzes & Posner's Five Leadership Practices model and Adair's Action-Centred Leadership theory assume that once the leader understands, and has been trained in, the required leadership behaviours, he or she will apply them as needed, regardless of their personality. However, as with the situational theories, Scouller noted that many cannot do so because of hidden beliefs and old habits so again he argued that most leaders may need to master their inner psychology if they are to adopt unfamiliar behaviours at will.

Leadership presence: The best leaders usually have something beyond their behaviour – something distinctive that commands attention, wins people's trust and enables them to lead successfully, which is often called 'leadership presence' (Scouller, 2011). This is possibly why the traits approach became researchers' original line of investigation into the sources of a leader's effectiveness. However, that that presence varies from person to person and research has shown it is hard to define in terms of common personality characteristics, so the traits approach failed to capture the elusive phenomenon of presence. The other key leadership theories do not address the nature and development of presence.

The three levels referred to in the model's name are Public, Private and Personal leadership. The model is usually presented in diagram form as three concentric circles and four outwardly directed arrows, with personal leadership in the centre.

> The first two levels – public and private leadership – are 'outer' or 'behavioural' levels. Scouller distinguished between the behaviours involved in influencing two or more people simultaneously When a leader is influencing more than one person simultaneously it called public leadership, but when it's one to one it's called private leadership. He listed thirty-four distinct public leadership behaviours and a further fourteen private leadership behaviours.

> The third level, personal leadership, is an 'inner' level and concerns a person's leadership presence, knowhow, skills, beliefs, emotions and unconscious habits. "At its heart is the leader's self-awareness, his progress toward self-mastery and technical competence, and his sense of connection with those around him. It's the inner core, the source, of a leader's outer leadership effectiveness" (Scouller 2011).

The idea is that if leaders want to be effective, they must work on all three levels in parallel.

The two outer levels, public and private leadership, are what the leader must do behaviourally with individuals or groups to address the 'four dimensions of leadership', which are:

a. A shared, motivating group purpose or vision.

b. Action, progress and results.

c. Collective unity or team spirit.

d. Individual selection and motivation.

The inner level, personal leadership, refers to what leaders should do to grow their leadership presence, knowhow and skill. It has three aspects:

a. Developing one's technical knowhow and skill.

b. Cultivating the right attitude toward other people.

c. Working on psychological self-mastery.

Scouller argued that self-mastery is the key to growing one's leadership presence, building trusting relationships with followers and enabling behavioural flexibility as circumstances change, while staying connected to one's core values. That is, while remaining authentic.

The assumption in this model is that personal leadership is the most powerful of the three levels. Scouller likened its effect to dropping a pebble in a pond and seeing the ripples spreading out from the centre, hence the four arrows pointing outward in the diagram: "The pebble represents inner, personal leadership and the ripples the two outer levels. Helpful inner change and growth will affect outer leadership positively. Negative inner change will cause the opposite."

a. PUBLIC LEADERSHIP

Public leadership refers to the actions or behaviours that leaders take to influence two or more people simultaneously, perhaps in a meeting or when addressing a large group. Public leadership is directed towards setting and agreeing on a motivating vision or future for the group or organisation to ensure unity of purpose. It is creating peer pressure towards shared, high-performance standards and an atmosphere of trust and team spirit; and driving successful collective action and results. Public leadership therefore serves the first three dimensions of leadership mentioned in the overview section.

There are thirty-four distinct public leadership behaviours, which break down as follows:

- o Setting the vision, staying focused: four behaviours.

- o Organizing, planning, giving power to others: two behaviours.

- o Ideation, problem-solving, decision-making: ten behaviours.

- o Executing: six behaviours

- o Group building and maintenance: twelve behaviours.

Leaders need to balance their time between the twenty-two vision/planning/thinking/execution behaviours, and the remaining twelve group building and maintenance behaviours.

According to the Three Levels of Leadership model, the key to widening one's repertoire of public leadership behaviours (and the skill with which they are performed) is attention to personal leadership.

b. PRIVATE LEADERSHIP

Private leadership concerns the leader's one-to-one handling of individuals which is the fourth and final dimension of leadership according to Scouller's theory. Although leadership involves creating a sense of group unity, groups are composed of individuals, and they vary in their ambitions, confidence, experience and psychological make-up. Therefore, they must be treated as individuals – hence the importance of *private* personal leadership. There are fourteen private leadership behaviours:

- o Individual purpose and task (e.g., appraising, selecting, disciplining): five behaviours.

- o Individual building and maintenance (e.g., recognizing rising talent): nine behaviours.

Some people experience the powerful conversations demanded by private leadership (e.g., performance appraisals) as uncomfortable. Consequently, leaders may avoid some of the private leadership behaviours, which reduces their leadership effectiveness. Scouller argued that the intimacy of private leadership leads to avoidant behaviour either because of a lack of skill or because of negative self-image beliefs that give rise to powerful fears of what may happen in such encounters. This is why personal leadership is so important in improving a leader's one-to-one skill and reducing his or her interpersonal fears.

c. PERSONAL LEADERSHIP

Personal leadership addresses the leader's technical, psychological and moral development and its impact on his or her leadership presence, skill and behaviour. It is, essentially, the key to making the theory of the two outer behavioural levels practical. Scouller went further in suggesting in the preface of his book, *The Three Levels of Leadership*, that personal leadership is the answer to what Jim Collins called "the inner development of a person to level 5 leadership" in the book *Good to Great*, something that Collins admitted he was unable to explain Bass 27). Personal leadership has three elements:

- Technical knowhow and skill.
- The right attitude towards other people; and
- Psychological self-mastery.

The first element, Technical Knowhow and Skill, is about knowing one's technical weaknesses and taking action to update one's knowledge and skills. Scouller suggested that there are three areas of knowhow that all leaders should learn: time management, individual psychology and group psychology. He also described the six sets of skills that underlie the public and private leadership behaviours:

- Group problem-solving and planning.
- Group decision-making.
- Interpersonal ability, which has a strong overlap with emotional intelligence.
- Managing group process.
- Assertiveness.
- Goal setting.

The second element, 'Attitude Toward Others', is about developing the right attitude toward colleagues in order to maintain the leader's relationships throughout the group's journey to its shared vision or goal. The right attitude is to believe that other people are as important as oneself and see leadership as an act of service. Although there is a moral aspect to this, there is also a practical side, for a leader's attitude and behaviour toward others will largely influence how much they respect and trust that person and want to work with him or her. Scouller outlined the five parts of the right attitude toward others:

- Interdependence.
- Appreciation.

- Caring.
- Service.
- Balance.

The two keys, he suggested, to developing these five aspects are to ensure that:

- There is a demanding, distinctive, shared vision that everyone in the group cares about and wants to achieve.
- The leader works on self-mastery to reduce self-esteem issues that make it hard to connect with, appreciate and adopt an attitude of service towards colleagues.

The third element of personal leadership is 'Self-Mastery'. It emphasises self-awareness and flexible command of one's mind, which allows the leader to let go of previously unconscious limiting beliefs and their associated defensive habits like avoiding powerful conversations, for example, appraisal discussions. It also enables leaders to connect more strongly with their values, let their leadership presence flow and act authentically in serving those they lead.

Because self-mastery is a psychological process, Scouller proposed a new model of the human psyche to support its practice. In addition, he outlined the principles of, and obstacles to, personal change and proposed six self-mastery techniques, which include mindfulness meditation.

3.7 LEADERSHIP PRESENCE

The importance and development of leadership presence is a central feature of the Three Levels of Leadership model. Scouller suggested that it takes more than the right knowhow, skills and behaviours to lead well, that it also demands *presence*. Presence has been summed up in this way:

At its root, it is wholeness. Presence is the rare but attainable inner alignment of self-identity, purpose and feelings that eventually leads to freedom from fear. It reveals itself as the magnetic, radiating effect you have on others when you're being the authentic *you*, giving them your full respect and attention, speaking honestly and letting your unique character traits flow. As leaders, we must be technically competent to gain others' respect, but it's our unique genuine presence that inspires people and prompts them to trust us; to want us as their leader.

In the Three Levels of Leadership model, presence is not the same as 'charisma'. Scouller argued that leaders can be charismatic by relying on a job title, fame, skilful acting or by the projection of an aura of 'specialness' by followers. Presence is something deeper, more authentic, more fundamental and more powerful and does not depend on social status. He contrasted the mental and moral resilience of a person with real presence with the susceptibility to pressure and immoral actions of someone whose charisma rests only on acting skills and the power their followers give them, not their true inner qualities.

Scouller also suggested that each person's authentic presence is unique and outlined seven qualities of presence:

- Personal power – command over one's thoughts, feelings and actions.
- High, real self-esteem.
- The drive to be more, to learn, to grow.
- A balance of an energetic sense of purpose with a concern for the service of others and respect for their free will.
- Intuition.
- Being in the now.
- Inner peace of mind and a sense of fulfillment.

Presence, according to this model, is developed by practicing personal leadership.

LINK WITH AUTHENTIC LEADERSHIP AND SERVANT LEADERSHIP

True leadership presence is, as Scouller defines it, synonymous with authenticity, being genuine and expressing one's highest values and an attitude of service towards those being led. So, in proposing self-mastery and cultivation of the right attitude toward others as a method of developing leadership presence, his model offers a 'how to' counterpart to the ideas of 'Authentic leadership' and 'servant leadership'.

- o **Authentic leadership** is an approach to leadership that emphasises building the leader's legitimacy through honest relationships with followers which value their input and are built on an ethical foundation. Generally, authentic leaders are positive people with truthful self-concepts who promote openness. By building trust and generating enthusiastic support from their subordinates, authentic leaders can improve individual and team performance. This approach has been fully embraced by many leaders and leadership coaches who view authentic leadership as an alternative to leaders who emphasise profit and share price over people and ethics. Authentic leadership is a growing area of study in academic research on leadership which has recently grown from obscurity to the beginnings of a fully mature concept. That said, many foundational papers on this topic have recently been retracted or called into question because of issues surrounding the reporting of data and the inability of the authors to produce their original data.

- o **Servant leadership** is a leadership philosophy. Traditional leadership generally involves the exercise of power by one at the 'top of the pyramid'. By comparison, the servant-leader shares power, puts the needs of others first and helps people develop and perform as highly as possible. Servant leadership turns the power pyramid upside down; instead of the people working to serve the leader, the leader exists to serve the people. When leaders shift their mindset and serve first, they unlock purpose and ingenuity in those around them, resulting in higher performance and engaged, fulfilled employees (Daft, Lengel 53).

SHARED LEADERSHIP

Most traditional theories of leadership explicitly or implicitly promote the idea of the leader as the admired hero, the person with all the answers that people want to follow. The Three Levels of Leadership model shifts away from this view. It does not reject the possibility of an impressive heroic leader, but it promotes the idea that this is only one way of leading, and, indeed, following, and that shared leadership is more realistic.

Shared leadership is a leadership style that broadly distributes leadership responsibility, such that people within a team and organization lead each other. It has frequently been compared to horizontal leadership, distributed leadership, and collective leadership and is most contrasted with more traditional 'vertical' or 'hierarchical' leadership that resides predominantly with an individual instead of a group (Daft, Lengel).

This view stems from Scouller's position that leadership is a process, "a series of choices and actions around defining and achieving a goal". Therefore, in his view, "leadership is a practical challenge that's bigger than the leader." He pointed out the danger of confusing leadership with the role of leader. As other authors such as John Adair have pointed out, leadership does not have to rely on one person because anyone in a group can exert leadership. Scouller went further to suggest that "not only can others exert leadership; they must exert it at times if a group is to be successful." In other words, he believed that shared rather than solo leadership is not an idealistic aspiration, but a matter of practicality. He suggested three reasons for this:

a. The sheer number of different behaviours required of leaders means they are unlikely to be equally proficient at all of them, so it is sensible for them to draw on their colleagues' strengths that is, to allow them to lead at times.

b. It is foolish to make one person responsible for all of leadership behaviours as it is likely to overburden them and frustrate any colleagues who are willing and able to lead in certain circumstances.

c. Shared leadership means that more people are involved in the group's big decisions, and this promotes joint accountability which, as Katzenbach & Smith found in their research, is a distinct feature of high-performance teams. (Katzenbach, Smith).

Now, potentially, this leaves the leader's role unclear. After all, if anyone in a group can lead, what is the distinct purpose of the leader? Scouller said this of the leader's role: "The purpose of a leader is to make sure there is leadership ... to ensure that all four dimensions of leadership are being addressed." The four dimensions being:

a. A shared, motivating group purpose or vision.

b. Action, progress and results.

c. Collective unity or team spirit.

d. Attention to individuals.

For example, the leader must ensure that there is a motivating vision or goal, but that does not mean he or she must supply the vision on their own. That is certainly one way of leading, but it is not the only way. Another way is to co-create the vision with one's colleagues.

This means that the leader can delegate, or share, part of the responsibility for leadership. However, the final responsibility for making sure that all four dimensions are covered still rests with the leader. So, although leaders can let someone else lead in a particular situation, they cannot let go of responsibility to make sure there is leadership. When the situation changes the leader must decide whether to take charge personally or pass situational responsibility to someone else.

One criticism of the Three Levels of Leadership model has been that it may be difficult for some leaders to use it as a guide to self-development without the assistance of a professional coach or psychotherapist at some point. This is because many of its ideas around self-mastery are deeply psychological.

CORE LEADERSHIP THEORIES

Why are some leaders successful, while others fail? The truth is that there is no magic combination of characteristics that makes leaders successful. Different characteristics matter in different circumstances. This doesn't mean, however, that you can't learn to be an effective leader. You just need to understand the various approaches to leadership, so that you can use the right approach for your situation.

One way of doing this is to learn about the core leadership theories that provide the backbone of our current understanding of leadership.

THE FOUR CORE THEORY GROUPS

Let's look at each of the four core groups of theory and explore some of the tools and models that apply with each. Keep in mind there are many other theories out there.

1. Trait Theories – What Type of Person Makes a Good Leader?
Trait theories argue that effective leaders share several common personalities, characteristics, or 'traits.'

Early trait theories said that leadership is an innate, instinctive quality that you do or don't have. Thankfully, we've moved on from this idea, and we're learning more about what we can do to develop leadership qualities within ourselves and others.

Trait theories help us identify traits and qualities that are helpful when leading others. For example, integrity, empathy, assertiveness, good decision-making skills, and likability. However, none of these traits, nor any specific combination of them, will guarantee success as a leader.

Traits are external behaviours that emerge from the things going on within our minds and it's these internal beliefs and processes that are important for effective leadership.

2. Behavioural Theories – What Does a Good Leader Do?
Behavioural theories focus on how leaders behave. For instance, do leaders dictate what needs to be done and expect cooperation? Or, do they involve their teams in decision making to encourage acceptance and support? In the 1930s, Kurt Lewin developed a framework based on a leader's behaviour. He argued that there are three types of leaders:

a. Autocratic leaders make decisions without consulting their teams. This style of leadership is considered appropriate when decisions need to be made quickly, when there's no need for input, and when team agreement isn't necessary for a successful outcome.

b. Authoritarian Leaders who get this rating are very much task oriented and are hard on their workers. There is little or no allowance for cooperation or collaboration. mostly display these characteristics: they are very strong on schedules; they expect people to do what they are told without question or debate. When something goes wrong, they tend to focus on who is to blame rather than concentrate on exactly what went wrong and how to prevent it. They are intolerant of what they see as dissent when it may just be someone's creativity, thus it is difficult for their subordinates to contribute or develop.

c. Democratic leaders allow the team to provide input before deciding, although the degree of input can vary from leader to leader. This style is important when team agreement matters, but it can be difficult to manage when there are lots of different perspectives and ideas.

d. Laissez-faire leaders don't interfere; they allow people within the team to make many of the decisions. This works well when the team is highly capable, motivated, and does not need close supervision. However, this behaviour can arise because the leader is lazy or distracted, and this is where this style of leadership can fail.

Clearly, how leaders behave affects their performance. Researchers have realised, though, that many of these leadership behaviours are appropriate at different times. The best leaders are those who can use many different behavioural styles and choose the right style for each situation.

3. Contingency Theories – How Does the Situation Influence Good Leadership?

The realisation that there is no one correct type of leader led to theories that the best leadership style depends on the situation. These theories try to predict which style is best in which circumstance.

4. Power and Influence Theories – What Is the Source of the Leader's Power?

Power and influence theories of leadership take an entirely different approach. These are based on the different ways that leaders use power and influence to get things done, and they look at the leadership styles that emerge as a result.

Perhaps the best-known of these theories is French and Raven's Five Forms of Power. This model highlights three types of positional power: legitimate, reward, and coercive, and two sources of personal power: expert and referent (your personal appeal and charm). This model suggests that using personal power is the better alternative, and that you should work on building expert power (the power that comes with being a real expert in the job) because this is the most legitimate source of personal power.

Another leadership style that uses power and influence is transactional leadership. This approach assumes that people do things for reward and for no other reason. Therefore, it focuses on designing tasks and reward structures. While this may not be the most appealing leadership strategy in terms of building relationships and developing a highly motivating work environment, it often works. Leaders in most organisations use it daily to get things done. Similarly, leading by example is another highly effective way of influencing your team.

EFFECTIVE LEADERSHIP STYLES

As we mentioned above, transformational leadership is often the best leadership style to use in business. Transformational leaders show integrity, and they know how to develop a robust and inspiring vision of the future. They motivate people to achieve this vision, manage its delivery, and build stronger and more successful teams. However, you'll often need to adapt your style to fit a specific group or situation, and this is why it's useful to gain a thorough understanding of other styles.

Transformational leadership is the most effective style to use in most business situations. However, you can become the tool and model associated with each one.

AUTHORITARIAN LEADER HIGH TASK, LOW RELATIONSHIP

Leaders who get this rating are very much task oriented and hard on their workers. There is little or no allowance for cooperation or collaboration. Authoritarian leaders mostly display these characteristics: they are very strong on schedules; they expect people to do what they are told without question or debate; when something goes wrong, they tend to focus on who is to blame rather than concentrate on exactly what went wrong and how to prevent it; they are intolerant of what they see as dissent (it may just be someone's creativity), thus it is difficult for their subordinates to contribute or develop.

TEAM LEADER HIGH TASK, HIGH RELATIONSHIP

These leaders lead by positive example and endeavour to foster a team environment so that all team members can reach their highest potential, both as individual team members and as a group of people who use cooperation and collaboration. They encourage the team to reach goals as effectively as possible, while also working tirelessly to strengthen the bonds among the various members. They normally lead some of the most productive teams.

WHAT IS WORLDVIEW AND HOW DOES IT AFFECT LEADERSHIP?

There are several definitions used for the term worldview, as it tends to be a concept more often dealt with in philosophy than the more typical academic and practical disciplines. A practical definition is that of James Sire: "A worldview is a set of presuppositions or assumptions which we hold consciously or unconsciously about the basic makeup of our world." (Sire 17). Phillips and Brown contend that "A Worldview is, first, an explanation and interpretation of the world and second, an application of this view to life. In simpler terms, our worldview is a view of the world, and a view for the world" (Phillips, Brown 29).

Another practical definition comes from wordIQ.com:

The English term worldview is a term derived from the German word Weltanschauung, one of the most important concepts in cognitive philosophy and generative sciences. This expression refers to the 'wide worldview' or 'wide world perception' of a people. The Weltanschauung of a people originates from the unique world experience of a people, which they experience over several millennia. The language of a people reflects the Weltanschauung of that people in the form of its structure. A world view describes a consistent and integral sense of existence and provides a framework for generating, sustaining and applying knowledge. The term denotes a comprehensive set of opinions, seen as an organic unity, about the world as the medium and exercise of human existence: politics, economics, religion, culture, science, and ethics. At all times, religious and political teachings were bases for forming worldviews. In fact, they were often worldviews themselves. For example, Christianity, Islam, socialism, Marxism, scientology may be called worldviews. At least, they generate clearly identifiable worldviews. Historically, world views changed little and slowly, achieving wide and often unquestioning support.

As should be apparent, worldview is an expansive concept; it is something we all have and ultimately frames how we view life. It is the framework that ties everything together, allows us to understand society, the world, and our place in it, and can help us make critical decisions which will shape our future.

F. Heylighen in the above referenced work attempts to explain the work of Leo Apostel, a Belgian philosopher and the work of many at the Centre Leo Apostel, an interdisciplinary research centre working on worldview. He describes the following seven components as fundamental to a worldview (Heylighen 1).

A MODEL OF THE WORLD

It should allow us to understand how the world functions and how it is structured. "'World' here means the totality, everything that exists around us, including the physical universe, Earth, life, mind, society and culture. We ourselves are an important part of that world. Therefore, a worldview should also answer the basic question, who are we?'

EXPLANATION

The second component is supposed to explain the first one. It should answer the questions: Why is the world the way it is? Where does it all come from? Where do we come from? This is perhaps the most important part of a worldview. If we can explain how and why a particular phenomenon, say life or mind, has arisen, we will be able to better understand how that phenomenon functions. It will also help us to understand how that phenomenon will continue to evolve.

FUTUROLOGY

This extrapolation of past evolution into the future defines a third component of a worldview: futurology. It should answer the question, 'Where are we going to?' It should give us a list of possibilities, of more or less probable future developments. This will confront us with a choice: which of the different alternatives should we promote, and which should we avoid?

VALUES

What it means for something to be good, or evil is the most fundamental issue of value. The theory of values defines the fourth component of a worldview. It includes morality, ethics, and the system of rules which tells us how we should or should not behave. It also gives us a sense of purpose, a direction or set of goals to guide our actions. Together with the answer to the question 'why?', the answer to the question 'what for?', may help us understand the real meaning of life.

ACTION

Knowing what to strive for does not yet mean knowing how to get there. The next component must be a theory of action. It would answer the question 'how should we act?' It helps us to solve practical problems and to implement plans of action.

KNOWLEDGE

Plans are based on knowledge and information, on theories and models describing the phenomena we encounter. Therefore, we need to understand how we can construct reliable models. This is the component of knowledge acquisition. It is equivalent to what in philosophy is called epistemology or 'the theory of knowledge'. It should allow us to distinguish better theories from worse theories. It should answer the traditional philosophic question: 'what is true and what is false?'

BUILDING BLOCKS

The final point on the agenda of a worldview builder is not meant to answer any fundamental question. It just reminds us that worldviews cannot be developed from scratch. You need building blocks to start with. These building blocks can be found in existing theories, models, concepts, guidelines and values, scattered over the different disciplines and ideologies. This defines the seventh component: fragments of worldviews as a starting point.

WHAT IS A CHRISTIAN WORLDVIEW?

The problem is immediate, and centres on the word Christian. Christianity is a broad cloth, with many doctrinal positions. As a result, most Christians develop worldviews primarily as a function of the culture they are raised in, the country they live in, or from their ethnic group or family. In many parts of Christianity, culture and faith are so closely tied (think Irish Catholic or Greek Orthodox), that the worldview is a mix of both.

Of note is that the American Fundamentalist-Evangelical movement has always been different, and through its history has focused on forming a specific worldview. For many years it was not a conscious undertaking, and worldview was probably not even in the lexicon of the movement. However, stemming out of the Biblical inerrancy and Biblical literacy beliefs were the foundational elements for a rigid and literalist worldview, one at increasing odds with science and common sense.

In the late 1990's, George Barna began defining and identifying Christian worldviews, and others began to focus on the subject as previously undefined need in Fundamentalist-Evangelical Christianity. Specifically, these people studied the concept enough to realise that the most effective way to shape and form Christians for life was to have an active role in the defining of their worldview.

Following some major public polling research in 2003, Barna said:

"Rather than simply providing people with good material and hoping they figure out what to do with it, these are churches whose services, programs, events and relationships are geared to weaving a limited number of foundational biblical principles into a way of responding to every life situation. The goal is to facilitate a means of interpreting and responding to every life situation that is consistent with God's expectations."

Thus, in the past two decades, an active undertaking came into being which began to create and solidify a Fundamentalist-Evangelical sub-culture through the definition of an acceptable worldview (Phillips, Brown 29).

An illuminating approach to this is the publication of the fundamentalist Probe Ministry, which begin with the assertion that all worldviews should be tested:

"A worldview should pass certain tests. First, it should be rational. It should not ask us to believe contradictory things. Second, it should be supported by evidence. It should be consistent with what we observe. Third, it should give a satisfying comprehensive explanation of reality. It should be able to explain why things are the way they are. Fourth, it should provide a satisfactory basis for living. It should not leave us feeling compelled to borrow elements of another worldview in order to live in this world" (Worldviews by Jerry Solomon, published by Probe Ministries, 1994).

They then go on to define what worldviews should necessarily contain:

"In addition to putting worldviews to these tests, we should also see that worldviews have common components. These four components are self-evident. It is important to keep these in mind as you establish your own worldview, and as you share with others. "

First, something exists. This may sound obvious, but it really is an important foundational element of worldview building since some will try to deny it. Denial is self- defeating because all people experience cause and effect. The universe is rational; it is predictable.

Second, all people have absolutes. Again, many will try to deny this, but somehow to deny it is to assert it. All of us seek an infinite reference point. For some it is God; for others it is the state, or love, or power, and for some this reference point is themselves or man.

Third, two contradictory statements cannot both be right. This is a primary law of logic that is continually denied. Ideally speaking, only one worldview can correctly mirror reality. This cannot be overemphasised considering the prominent belief that tolerance is the ultimate virtue. To say that someone is wrong is considered intolerant or narrow-minded. A good illustration of this is when we hear people declare that all religions are the same. It would mean that Hindus, for example, agree with Christians concerning God, Jesus, salvation, heaven, hell, and a host of other doctrines. This is nonsense.

Fourth, all people exercise faith. All of us presuppose certain things to be true without absolute proof. These are inferences or assumptions upon which a belief is based. This becomes important, for example, when we interact with those who allege that only the scientist is completely neutral. Some common assumptions are a personal God exists, man evolved from inorganic material, man is essentially good or else that reality is material.

As we converse with people who have opposing worldviews, an understanding of these common components can help us listen more patiently, and they can guide us to make our case more wisely.

The notion of "dialoguing with people who have opposing worldviews" makes it clear that there are two purposes at work. The first is to define your own worldview. The second is to convince others they should adopt yours.

How do you determine what is right and wrong? Often, we hear it said that ethics are relative or situational. Others assert that we have no free choice since we are entirely determined. Some simply derive 'ought' from what 'is'. Of course, history has shown us the tragic results of a 'might makes right' answer.

THE WORLDVIEW OUTCOME

Barna, Solomon and others in the Fundamentalist-Evangelical movement have come to the correct observation that worldview is among the most fundamental aspects of a person and how they view the world.

What they set out to do, however, is to define a worldview that is acceptable to the Fundamental-Evangelical faith position and then develop a methodology to inculcate that into 'the faithful'. The result is a group of believers who are very deeply and solidly grounded in a view of life despite, and often regardless, of the facts.

4. WHAT IS SERVANT LEARDERSHIP?

Servant leadership is a leadership philosophy. Traditional leadership generally involves t exercise of power by one at the "top of the pyramid." By comparison, the servant-leader shares power, puts the needs of others first and helps people develop and perform as highly as possible. Servant leadership turns the power pyramid upside down. Instead of people working to serve the leader, the latter exists to serve the people. When leaders shift their mindset and serve first, they unlock purpose and ingenuity in those around them, resulting in higher performance and engaged, fulfilled employees.

While the idea of servant leadership goes back at least two thousand years, the modern servant leadership movement was launched by Robert K. Greenleaf in 1970 with the publication of his classic essay, 'The Servant as Leader'. It was in this essay that he coined the words 'servant-leader' and 'servant leadership' (Greenleaf). Greenleaf defined the servant-leader as follows:

"The servant-leader is servant first... It begins with the natural feeling that one wants to serve, to serve first. Then conscious choice brings one to aspire to lead. That person is sharply different from one who is leader first, perhaps because of the need to satisfy an unusual power drive or to acquire material possessions... The leader-first and the servant-first are two extreme types. Between them there are shadings and blends that are part of the infinite variety of human nature."

The difference manifests itself in the care taken by the servant-first approach to make sure that other people's highest priority needs are being served. The best test, yet difficult to administer, is: "Do those served grow as people? Do they, while being served, become healthier, wiser, freer, more autonomous, more likely themselves to become servants? What is the effect on the least privileged in society? Will they benefit or at least not be further deprived?"

Greenleaf said that "the servant-leader is servant first." By that he meant that the desire to serve, in the 'servant's heart', is a fundamental characteristic of a servant-leader. It is not about being servile, it is about wanting to help others. It is about identifying and meeting the needs of colleagues, customers, and communities. The great leader is seen as servant first, and that simple fact is the key to his greatness.

If there is a single characteristic of the servant-leader that stands out in Greenleaf's essay, it is the desire to serve. A walk through The Servant as Leader provides a fairly long list of additional characteristics that Greenleaf considered important. They include listening and understanding; acceptance and empathy' foresight; awareness and perception; persuasion; conceptualisation; self-healing; and rebuilding community. Servant-leaders are people who initiate action, are goal-oriented, dreamers of great dreams, good communicators, can withdraw and re-orient themselves, and are dependable, trusted, creative, intuitive, and situational.

Scholars are identifying characteristics of servant leadership to develop and test theories about the impact of servant leadership. For example, Robert C. Liden and his colleagues identified nine dimensions of servant leadership that they used in their research: emotional healing, creating value for the community, conceptual skills, empowering, helping subordinates grow and succeed, putting subordinates first, behaving ethically, relationships, and servanthood (Linden, Liao, Meuser).

Dirk van Dierendonck reviewed the scholarly literature and identified six key characteristics of servant-leader behaviour: empowering and developing people, humility, authenticity, interpersonal acceptance, providing direction, and stewardship (Dierendonck).

Greenleaf described a philosophy, not a theory. However, based on the views of several scholars, the elements that are most unique to servant leadership compared with other theories are:

a. The moral component, not only in terms of personal morality and integrity of the servant-leader, but also in terms of the way in which a servant-leader encourages enhanced moral reasoning among his or her followers, who can therefore test the moral basis of the servant-leader's visions and organisational goals.

b. The focus on serving followers for their own good, not just the good of the organisation, and forming long-term relationships with followers, encouraging their growth and development so that over time they may reach their fullest potential.

c. Concern with the success of all stakeholders. Broadly defined, these include, employees, customers, business partners, communities, and society as a whole, including those who are the least privileged; and

d. Self-reflection, as a counter to the leader's hubris.

The phrase "servant leadership" may not be familiar to many individuals or organisations, but it is a belief system that is already widely embraced by some of the most successful organisations in the world. Its essence is a focus on individuals and a decentralised organisational structure. It also emphasises other core values that encourage innovation and the development of leaders that must first focus on serving all stakeholders in an organisation.

Below is a discussion of servant leadership and why it can be an important driver for entities and individuals that embrace its core concepts.

Servant leadership represents a decentralised structure that focuses on employee empowerment and encourages innovation. This means having upper management share key decision-making powers with employees who work directly with clients and customers; they are arguably better aware of what is needed to remain competitive because of their knowledge of what is occurring on the 'front lines' of the business.

The Greenleaf Centre explains that when companies are close to the customer, they make better decisions that both retain clients and win new ones. Overall, this system is "more efficient and effective in allocating resources". It also encourages innovation, which firms need to survive. Corporate cultures that centralise power in the wrong hands can end up stifling innovation.

Perhaps most importantly, servant leadership is focused on serving all stakeholders in the corporation. This includes employees, customers and the community in general. It is seen as an evolution of a traditional corporate measure that emphasises growing shareholder returns over time. A criticism of this measure is that it can be at the expense of the other stakeholders, especially if profit is the only driver of corporate success and leads to the trampling of other stakeholders that are vital to long-term survival of an organisation.

THE PRIMARY CHARACTERISTIC OF SERVANT LEADERSHIP

Larry Spears listed several essential characteristics that he saw as defining servant leadership (Spears). For firms to remain competitive, listening is crucial. Employees must stay connected to customers and industry developments and they need to listen and remain receptive to clients. This is because those external parties frequently have significant insight into product successes and changes that could grow into challenges or ruin a firm if not addressed. Additionally, persuasion is suggested through consensus-building and stands in direct contrast to tactics that are considered more about command and control. Coercive tactics that are pushed through from more centralised organisations can be especially destructive.

From an employee development perspective, empathy means adopting the point of view according to which both customers and colleagues have good intentions. It emphasises open-mindedness when considering decisions. Healing might seem too soft for many corporate cultures, but at its core it emphasises the development of individuals from both personal and professional perspectives. For instance, encouraging learning, development, and constructive feedback along with the completion of job tasks is the focus of this characteristic. Foresight is like awareness but stresses the ability to use past lessons for success going forward. A commitment to people's growth is also warranted, as is an emphasis on developing talent. At its best, servant leadership can help a firm run more effectively.

Servant leadership-oriented corporations take the stance that what is good for customers is good for business. Such a culture encourages employees to create products of high quality and value in terms of price and utility to consumers.

Firms that qualify as going against the concepts of servant leadership include those that fell by the wayside during the 2008 mortgage meltdown. Lehman Brothers and Bear Stearns are derided for placing greed and growth over customers that were sold sophisticated investment products for which they had little understanding or need. Employees, especially those in upper management, were unduly focused on profits and personal gain over a sustainable goal of treating all stakeholders with respect.

In essence, servant leadership has many useful concepts that can be applied to businesses to help them run more effectively and efficiently. For investors, it can be used to identify firms that have the best chances for success while operating in intensely competitive industries.

Servant leadership is obviously wary of a centralised, command-and-control style, but there are still going to be many instances where it is the most effective way to manage certain business operations. It's up to organisations to strike the right balance between centralised and decentralised activities. Overall, servant leadership is important for its holistic views of corporations, individuals and communities, and for teaching them how to protect and encourage their well-being.

The most common division of leadership styles is the distinction between autocratic, participative and servant leadership styles. The authoritarian style of leadership requires clearly defined tasks and monitoring their execution and results. The decision-making responsibility rests with the executive. In contrast to the autocratic, the practice of participative leadership involves employees in decision-making. More extensive tasks are delegated. The employees influence and responsibility increases. The unrestrictive style of leadership is negligible in practice.

Servant leadership can be most likely associated with the participative leadership style. The authoritarian leadership style does not correspond to the guiding principle. The highest priority of a servant leader is to encourage, support and enable subordinates to unfold their full potential and ability. This leads to an obligation to delegate responsibility and engage in participative decision-making, the participative style of leadership is presented as the approach with the greatest possible performance and employee satisfaction.

The servant leadership approach goes beyond employee-related behaviour and calls for a rethinking of the hierarchical relationship between leader and subordinates. This does not mean that the ideal of a participative style in any situation is to be enforced, but that the focus of leadership responsibility is the promotion of performance and satisfaction of employees.

Unlike leadership approaches with a top-down hierarchical style, servant leadership instead emphasises collaboration, trust, empathy, and the ethical use of power. At heart, the individual is a servant first, making the conscious decision to lead to better serve others, not to increase their own power. The objective is to enhance the growth of individuals in the organisation and increase teamwork and personal involvement. A recent behavioural economics experiment demonstrates the group benefits of servant leadership. Teams of players coordinated their actions better with a servant leader resulting in improved outcomes for the followers but not for the selfless leaders.

From the teaching and example of Jesus Christ we learn that being a servant leader in the most general sense means being:

- A voluntary servant, who submits themselves to a higher purpose, which is beyond their personal interests, or the interests of others.

- A leader who uses the power that is entrusted to them to serve others.

- A servant who, out of love, serves other's needs before their own.

- A teacher who teaches their followers, in word and deed, how to become servant leaders themselves.

The focus is on the growth of the individual that they might flourish and achieve their full potential and not primarily the growth and potential of the organisation, distinguishing servant leadership from other leadership styles. The primary concern of the servant leader is service to their followers.

In the secular business schools as mentioned before, it was Robert Greenleaf who, in the early 1970s, proposed the servant leader model. However, the concept of a servant leader is not such a modern concept but can be found in the biblical account of the life of Jesus Christ. By examining his model, we can identify a Christ-centred, Christ-like servant leadership style that works for Christians who lead people in any situation.

Servant leadership manifests itself in different ways in different organisations. For instance, the fun-loving antics of Southwest Airlines probably would not fit the more conservative culture of a major financial organisation like Synovus Financial Corporation. Yet both organisations base their organisational culture on the servant leadership principles articulated by Greenleaf. Both companies consistently appear in the Fortune '100 Best Companies to Work For' list, and both have been the number one company on the list in previous years (Barrett).

Some think that the servant leadership model is too soft and doesn't recognise the political nature of organisations and institutions. Nothing could be further from the truth. Where there is power there will always be politics. What the servant leadership model does is reshape the political environment so that political power is used to protect and build people, rather than keep them in a state of dependency. It deals with the reality of political power and its legitimate and ethical use. However, while protecting people from danger, servant leaders also expose them to a greater awareness of reality. That is why servant leadership can be so dangerous in some organisations. Challenging the power model of leadership is not just challenging a leadership style. It is challenging a worldview, and belief system, that provides control, consistency, and predictability to those in power.

John F. 'Jack' Welch (2009), chairman and CEO of General Electric for twenty years, and one of the most highly regarded leaders in the business world today, once said that management is "looking reality straight in the eye and then acting upon it with as much speed as you can" (Connors, Smith, Hickman). Robert Greenleaf said, "awareness is not a giver of solace it is just the opposite after solace. They have their own serenity."

Servant leadership involves a mature worldview that chooses service over self-interest. Mature people recognise joint accountability. Achieving a high level of interdependence requires a culture where leaders listen intently first with the purpose of understanding. The job of the servant leader is to listen, identify, and clarify what the organisation is saying. This level of listening requires more than just hearing. To the servant leader listening means a genuine willingness to be influenced by those you serve.

Servant leadership also involves developing an organisational culture that exhibits a high level of trust. Trust is dependent on having trustworthy people. Trustworthy people are principled and 'walk their talk'. Therefore, personal leadership success precedes organisational leadership success. Dr. Stephen Covey calls these two leadership successes the 'private victory' and 'public victory'. He says that private victories must precede public victories. This inside-out approach is captured in the saying; "I cannot call myself your servant until I can call myself my master." Self-mastery is essential for successful personal leadership (Covey 72). You cannot successfully lead others under the servant leadership model until you have first achieved a certain level of personal leadership mastery and internal synergy.

Practicing servant leadership within an organisation means performing acts which help people remove the obstacles in their way, and helping them acquire the tools and resources they need to do their jobs better. It means jumping into the trenches and being willing to do whatever it takes to get the job done. It means leading by example. It means lightening the load of another. It means being willing to do whatever you ask others to do. It means levelling hierarchies. It means not only being a boss, but also a friend. It means listening to those served to find out what they really need you to do for them, rather than deciding yourself what is best for them. Just because one serves, and has a leadership position, does not make that person a true servant leader, a true servant leader is servant first. Others may aspire first to become a leader and then to serve, or to aspire to serve in a manner that is patriarchal and controlling. A true servant leader, however, is one that exhibits very specific characteristics. Larry Spears, Executive Director of The Greenleaf Centre for Servant-Leadership, has identified 10 critical characteristics that a servant leader should exhibit. These ten are by no means complete but do communicate important aspects of this leadership model (Greenlea 105).

The ten characteristics are:

    a. Listening

    b. Empathy

    c. Healing

    d. Awareness

    e. Persuasion

    f. Conceptualisation

    g. Foresight

    h. Stewardship

    i. Commitment to the growth of people

    j. Building community

In describing servant leadership to another, it is recognised that the listener is always filtering and interpreting what is being said based on their current worldview. Truly understanding the servant leadership model may require a paradigm shift from old ways of thinking. It may require discarding old assumptions. It may require viewing the world differently. To accomplish this, it will be necessary to be vulnerable, to listen for understanding, to respect differences in perspective, and to receive personal feedback from others. Only then will you be able to effectively examine and modify your assumptions, values, and paradigms (your worldview).

The servant leadership model cannot be achieved with a 'quick fix' approach. It cannot be instilled quickly within an organisation. The transformation of the worldviews of individuals that make up an organisation is a long-term, continuous effort. The decision to pursue the servant leadership model is certainly a matter of organisational strategy, but at its core, it is a matter of personal choice.

Is servant leadership a part of your worldview?

Applying these considerations of Jesus as a role model for Christian leaders we can see that, from a Biblical perspective, a servant leader is a person, who is:

- Christ-centred in all aspects of life; a voluntary servant of Christ.
- Committed to serve the needs of others before their own.
- Courageous to lead with power and love as an expression of serving.
- Consistently developing others into servant leaders.
- Continually inviting feedback from those that they want to serve so as to grow towards the ultimate servant leader, Jesus Christ.

There are some noteworthy implications that arise:

The servant leader is a 'servant in all things' in relationship to God. This is the Christian servant leader's higher purpose. He is also a 'servant first' in relationship to people. Jesus Christ came into this world as God's servant (Isaiah 42:1, Isaiah 52:13, Acts 3:26, 4:27). He also came to serve man (Matthew 20:28). However, Christ did not come to be our servant, whereas he came out of obedience to God, serving him.

Christians are called to be God's servants in every aspect of our lives. From the Bible it's clear that this means serving fellow man in accordance with the higher purpose of serving God. Note, however, that simply serving people is insufficient. It does not necessarily imply that a leader is serving God. It is possible, for instance, to serve people based on a humanistic worldview. There is a big difference between serving the needs of others and being a servant of others' needs.

Serving the needs of others is liberating. It implies recognising their needs without judging them, and then doing what can be done, in line with the higher purpose of serving God first, to help satisfy that need. Whereas being a servant of the needs of others, requires that one must do anything and everything possible to satisfy those needs, whether it is in line with one's service to God or not.

The servant leader themselves is a growing leader, led and grown by the Holy Spirit.

Jesus was the only human being who never abused his power. For a leader the abuse of power is a major issue and temptation. The keys to avoiding abuse of power are feedback from God and the followers, along with sharing power. These factors are necessary to help the leader apply power in line with God's purpose and in the best interests of the followers. The development and growth of followers into servant leaders inherently requires that the servant leader passes power on to them (sharing power), so that they can also grow in using that power to serve others according to the higher purpose.

4. WHAT IS SERVANT LEADERSHIP?

Servant leadership is more about being than doing.

Without a serving heart it is almost impossible to become a servant leader. While servant leadership is a timeless concept, there are different ways to grow servant leaders, although Greenleaf (the founder of secular servant leadership) considers that a leader may need a "conversion experience" to become a servant leader. In any event, the highest priority should be given to help servant leaders to grow in their service to God. Out of the service to God, true service to others flows more easily.

What should a Christian leader be like?

There is no finer example for Christian leadership than our Lord Jesus Christ. He declared: "I am the good shepherd. The good shepherd lays down his life for the sheep" (**John 10:11**). It is within this verse that we see the perfect description of a Christian leader. He is one who acts as a shepherd to those 'sheep' in his care.

When Jesus referred to us as 'sheep', He was not speaking in affectionate terms. In truth, sheep rank among the dumbest animals in creation. A stray sheep, still within earshot of the herd, becomes disoriented, confused, frightened, and incapable of finding its way back to the flock. Unable to ward off hungry predators, the stray is perhaps the most helpless of all creatures. Entire herds of sheep are known to have drowned during times of flash flooding even in sight of easily accessible higher ground. Like it or not, when Jesus called us His sheep, He was saying that without a shepherd, we are helpless.

The shepherd is one who has several roles regarding his sheep. He leads, feeds, nurtures, comforts, corrects and protects them. The shepherd of the Lord's flock leads by modelling godliness and righteousness in his own life and encouraging others to follow his example. Of course, our ultimate example, and the One we should follow, is Christ Himself. The Apostle Paul understood this: "Follow my example, as I follow the example of Christ" (1 Corinthians 11:1). The Christian leader is one who follows Christ and inspires others to follow Him as well.

The Christian leader is also a feeder and a nourisher of the sheep, and the ultimate 'sheep food' is the Word of God. Just as the shepherd leads his flock to the richest pasture so they will grow and flourish, so the Christian leader nourishes his flock with the only food which will produce strong, vibrant Christians. The Bible, not psychology or the world's wisdom, is the only diet that can produce healthy Christians. "Man does not live on bread alone but on every word that comes from the mouth of the Lord" (Deuteronomy 8:3).

The Christian leader also comforts the sheep, binding up their wounds and applying the balm of compassion and love. As the great Shepherd of Israel, the Lord Himself promised to "bind up the injured and strengthen the weak" (**Ezekiel 34:16**). As Christians in the world today, we suffer many injuries to our souls, and we need compassionate leaders who will bear our burdens with us, sympathise with our circumstances, exhibit patience toward us, encourage us in the Word, and bring our concerns before the Father's throne.

Just as the shepherd used his crook to pull a wandering sheep back into the fold, so the Christian leader corrects and disciplines those in his care when they go astray. Without rancour or an overbearing spirit, but with a "spirit of gentleness" (**Galatians 6:1-2**), those in leadership must correct according to scriptural principles. Correction or discipline is never a pleasant experience for either party, but the Christian leader who fails in this area is not exhibiting love for those in his care. "The Lord disciplines those he loves" (**Proverbs 3:12**), and the Christian leader must follow His example.

The final role of the Christian leader is that of a protector. The shepherd who was lax in this area soon found that he regularly lost sheep to the predators who prowled around, and sometimes among, his flock. The predators today are those who try to lure the sheep away with false doctrine, dismissing the Bible as quaint and old fashioned, insufficient, unclear, or unknowable. These lies are spread by those against whom Jesus warned us: "Watch out for false prophets. They come to you in sheep's clothing, but inwardly they are ferocious wolves" (**Matthew 7:15**). Our leaders must protect us from the false teachings of those who would lead us astray from the truth of the Scripture and the fact that Christ alone is the way of salvation: "I am the way, the truth, and the life. No one comes to the Father except through Me" (**John 14:6**).

Under the plan God has ordained for the church, leadership is a position of humble and loving service. Church leadership is ministry, not management. Those whom God designates as leaders are called not to be governing monarchs, but humble slaves, not slick celebrities, but labouring servants. Those who would lead God's people must above all exemplify sacrifice, devotion, submission, and lowliness. Jesus Himself gave us the pattern when He stooped to wash His disciples' feet, a task that was customarily done by the lowest of slaves (John 13). If the Lord of the universe would do that, no church leader has a right to think of himself as a big boss.

Any discussion of great leaders will include the cliché that the best leaders lead by example. Stated in conversation, everyone will nod and agree. If you are reflecting personally on the attributes of those you have willingly followed, you will find that common trait too. It seems there is little doubt that we influence others through our actions, especially when we are in a leadership role.

The challenge is that it isn't just great leaders who are leading by example, we all are. As a leader, supervisor, or manager, people are watching us. They are noticing everything we do, whether it is what we would want them to emulate, or not. Since people are watching and are influenced by our behaviour, for better or worse, it begs a very important question:

What is the example we want to be setting?

This might seem like a simple question, but I have found that in practice, it isn't quite that clear, and even when it is, it is not all that easy. If your vision of 'leading by example' is creating some sort of cadre of mini versions of yourself, you are misguided. It won't really create the results you desire, even if your behaviours are fully worthy of being followed.

What leading by example' should mean is that our actions influence others to behave and respond in ways that we deem valuable and appropriate for our organisational outcomes. In other words, while we need to focus on our behaviours, it isn't for ego purposes, but for the organisation's benefit. This is also made more difficult because we have a hard time describing what we really want from others. We talk in high level, vague language that is very difficult to turn into behaviours that can be emulated by others. The hit parade of attributes people says they want in team members includes:

- Engaged and empowered.
- Flexible and open to change.
- Focused.
- Good attitude.
- Good work ethic.

This is a good list, but what do these things really mean as we work every day?

If you can't answer that question clearly, you can't lead by example because you don't know what the example is supposed to be. In other words, if we are going to lead by example in relation to that list, we need to know what we really mean, and determine what behaviours create those outcomes. To answer the question implied in the title, let's examine the example as it relates to the five items on the list above.

Because of what these things mean, they matter even more in your organisation. Your ownership of these ideas and behaviours makes a difference.

If you want engagement and empowerment, consider the following behaviours:

- o Act like an owner – make decisions based on the highest good for the business and objectives.
- o Be proactive by asking what you can do to help or improve a situation.
- o Be accountable, recognising that there is always part of the project or result that you can impact in a positive way.
- o Try things in service of the desired goal. If you make a mistake, own it, and learn from it.

While this is just a partial list, it shows how to translate those principles into action. When the team members are engaged and empowered, they are doing these things.

Below, a few of the key differences are outlines:

- o Gets you to think and clarify what you are looking for from your team.
- o Gets you to look in the mirror and see if you are delivering those things personally.
- o Gives you a process for translating what you want into the behaviours that produce it.

The 'lead by example' cliché is called so because it is true; people are influenced by our actions. Our life as a leader would be easier if we could say all the right things and know that those words would significantly influence our team. While that would be easier, it is also unrealistic. While our words matter, what we do matters far more. Put another way, others watch our feet more than our lips. If we want our influence to be positive and productive, we must be clear on what we want from others, and then make sure our actions, as well as our words, support that. When we do this, we are leading by example in an intentional and productive way.

7 THINGS GREAT LEADERS ALWAYS DO BUT MERE MANAGERS ALWAYS FEAR

There are a lot of differences between a great leader and a mere manager. Just because they call someone a manager does not mean they get to be a leader. In some organisations, almost anyone can get promoted to management if they put in the time and play the right politics. Instead of trying to become a mere manager, why not aspire to become a great leader? Here are a few of the key differences.

A GREAT LEADER CONNECTS DAILY WORK WITH GREAT GOALS. A MERE MANAGER FOCUSES ONLY ON THE SHORT-TERM

It's easy to get caught focusing on things that are urgent, rather than important. A mere manager spends most energy on the daily grind, and harangues his people for not achieving short-term goals, regardless of their long-term importance. A truly great leader on the other hand, could hardly care less about Transaction Processing System (TPS) reports, or whatever the equivalent is in his or her workplace, and probably must work to hide his or her contempt for such bureaucratic goofiness. What matters most to him or her is what matters most.

A GREAT LEADER THINKS OF PEOPLE AS PEOPLE. A MERE MANAGER SEES ONLY TITLES OR ORGANISATIONAL CHARTS

If you catch yourself referring to people on your team by their job titles as often as by their names, beware you're on the road to becoming more of a manager than a leader. A real leader thinks of people individually and holistically, and tries hard to understand strengths and weaknesses, goals and interests.

In the military, for example, great leaders grow to know their soldiers, and lesser leaders refer to them generically, either by their ranks or occupational specialties. There might be nothing less dehumanising to hear than an officer refer to his troops as a bunch of '11-Bang-Bangs' (slang for '11-Bravo', which is in turn the bureaucratic designation for an infantry soldier).

A GREAT LEADER WANTS TO EARN RESPECT. A MERE MANAGER WANTS TO BE LIKED

Great leaders aren't always the most likable people. In the long run, great leaders recognise that their job is to get people to do things they might not want to do, in order to achieve goals they want to achieve. Contrast that with mere managers, who either want to be liked or try to convince themselves that they don't care. Great leaders know that cordiality is necessary, but also that they might sometimes have to sacrifice short-term likability in favour of long-term respect.

A REAL LEADER IS THRILLED WHEN TEAM MEMBERS ACHIEVE GREAT THINGS. A MERE MANAGER IS THREATENED

In the grand scheme of things, a mere manager doesn't have much. He or she has not aspired to enough in life and has taken on a bureaucratic role. Yet that's all he or she has, and as a result, the fear of losing it can be overwhelming. Thus, when a team member outgrows her role, a manager worries first about being outshone. A true leader, on the other hand, takes his or her team members' accomplishments as a point of pride, and recognises that the mark of a great leader isn't creating followers, but developing new leaders.

A GREAT LEADER EMPOWERS PEOPLE WITH HONESTY AND TRANSPARENCY. A MERE MANAGER PARCELS OUT INFORMATION AS IF IT COSTS HIM PERSONALLY

We have all likely seen this issue firsthand. A great leader understands that all else being equal, transparency shows respect for your team and helps them do good work. A mere manager, however, fears that sharing information can be tantamount to giving up leverage. So, he or she holds their cards close to their chest and undermines the team's performance in the process.

A GREAT LEADER UNDERSTANDS THAT IF THE TEAM FALLS SHORT, HE IS RESPONSIBLE. A MERE MANAGER BLAMES THE TEAM

Once more, it all comes down to fear. A mere manager hasn't earned anyone's respect, so he or she is constantly afraid of losing power. If the team doesn't accomplish its goals, the mere manager is primarily concerned about losing his or her role on an organisational hierarchy. A true leader, on the other hand, recognises that no matter the reason why the team falls short, he or she is to blame. Even if he or she believes that a specific team member might have been the cause, a true leader shoulders the blame and spurs the team to do better.

A GREAT LEADER CARES MAINLY ABOUT RESULTS. A MERE MANAGER IS MORE CONCERNED WITH PROCESS

To be fair, some organisations' management positions are designed to protect processes, not to empower people. Seriously, who cares about process when the results are positive? You might also realise that this puts you in the minority of leaders. Regardless, the main rule that a true leader lives by is that it's better to be resourceful, and that it's always easier to get forgiveness than permission (Murphy).

5. WHAT JESUS HAS TO SAY ON LEADERSHIP

Jesus submitted his own life to sacrificial service under the will of God:

> "Father, if you are willing, take this cup from me; yet not my will, but yours be done" (Luke 22:42).

He sacrificed his life freely out of service for others:

> "I and The Father are one" (John 10:30).

He came to serve:

> "Just as the Son of Man did not come to be served, but to serve, and to give his life as a ransom for many" (Matthew 20:28).

Although he was God's son and was thus more powerful than any other leader in the world. He healed the sick:

> "Then Jesus left the vicinity of Tyre and went through Sidon, down to the Sea of Galilee and into the region of the Decapolis. There some people brought to him a man who was deaf and could hardly talk, and they

begged Jesus to place his hand on him. After he took him aside, away from the crowd, Jesus put his fingers into the man's ears. Then he spit and touched the man's tongue. He looked up to heaven and with a deep sigh said to him, "Ephphatha!" (which means "Be opened!"). At this, the man's ears were opened, his tongue was loosened, and he began to speak plainly. Jesus commanded them not to tell anyone. But the more he did so, the more they kept talking about it. People were overwhelmed with amazement. "He has done everything well," they said. "He even makes the deaf hear and the mute speak." (Mark 7:31-37).

He drove out demons:

"They went across the lake to the region of the Gerasene. And When Jesus got out of the boat, a man with an impure spirit came from the tombs to meet him. This man lived in the tombs, and no one could bind him anymore, not even with a chain. For he had often been chained hand and foot, but he tore the chains apart and broke the irons on his feet. No one was strong enough to subdue him. Night and day among the tombs and in the hills, he would cry out and cut himself with stones. When he saw Jesus from a distance, he ran and fell on his knees in front of him. He shouted at the top of his voice, "What do you want with me, Jesus, Son of the most High God? In God's name don't torture me!" For Jesus had said to him, "Come out of this man, you impure spirit!" Then Jesus asked him, "What is your name?" "My name is Legion," he replied, "for we are many." And he begged Jesus again and again not to send them out of the area. A large herd of pigs was feeding on the nearby hillside. The demons begged Jesus, "Send us among the pigs; allow us to go into them." He gave them permission, and the impure spirits came out and went into the pigs. The herd, about two thousand in number, rushed down the steep bank into the lake and were drowned. Those tending the pigs ran off and reported this in the town and countryside, and the people went out to see what had happened. When they came to Jesus, they saw the man who had been possessed by the legion of demons, sitting there, dressed and in his right mind; and they were afraid. Those who had seen it told the people what had happened to the demon-possessed man—and told them about the pigs as well. Then the people began to plead with Jesus to leave their region. As Jesus was getting into the boat, the man who had been demon-possessed begged to go with him. Jesus did not let him, but said, "Go home to your own people and tell them how much the Lord has done for you, and how he has had mercy on you." So, the man went away and began to tell in the Decapolis how much Jesus had done for him. And all the people were amazed" (Mark 5:1-20).

He was recognised as Teacher and Lord:

"You call me 'Teacher' and 'Lord,' and rightly so, for that is what I am" (John 13:13).

He had power over the wind, the sea and even over death:

"That day when evening came, he said to his disciples, "Let us go over to the other side." Leaving the crowd behind, they took him along, just as he was, in the boat. There were also other boats with him. A furious squall came up, and the waves broke over the boat, so that it was nearly swamped. Jesús was in the stern, sleeping on a cushion. The disciples woke him and said to him, "Teacher, don't you care if we drown?" He got up, rebuked the wind and said to the waves, "Quiet! Be still!" Then the wind died down and it was completely calm. He said to his disciples, "Why are you so afraid? Do you still have no faith?" They were terrified and asked each other, "Who is this? Even the wind and the waves obey him!" (Mark 4:35-41)

"While he was saying this, a synagogue leader came and knelt before him and said, "My daughter has just died. But come and put your hand on her, and she will live." Jesus got up and went with him, and so did his disciples. Just then a woman who had been subject to bleeding for twelve years came up behind him and touched the edge of his cloak. She said to herself, "If I only touch his cloak, I will be healed." Jesus turned and saw her. "Take heart, daughter," he said, "your faith has healed you." And the woman was healed at that moment. When Jesus entered the synagogue leader's house and saw the noisy crowd and people playing pipes, he said, "Go away. The girl is not dead but asleep." But they laughed at him. After the crowd had been put outside, he went in and took the girl by the hand, and she got up. News of this spread through all that region." (Matthew 9:18-26).

In John 13:1-17, Jesus gives a very practical example of what it means to serve:

"It was just before the Passover Festival. Jesus knew that the hour had come for him to leave this world and go to the Father. Having loved his own who were in the world, he loved them to the end. The evening meal was in progress, and the devil had already prompted Judas, the son of Simon Iscariot, to betray Jesus. Jesus knew that the Father had put all things under his power, and that he had come from God and was returning to

God; so, he got up from the meal, took off his outer clothing, and wrapped a towel around his waist. After that, he poured water into a basin and began to wash his disciples' feet, drying them with the towel that was wrapped around him. He came to Simon Peter, who said to him, "Lord, are you going to wash my feet?" Jesus replied, "You do not realise now what I am doing, but later you will understand." "No," said Peter, "you shall never wash my feet." Jesus answered, "Unless I wash you, you have no part with me."

"Then, Lord," Simon Peter replied, "not just my feet but my hands and my head as well!" Jesus answered, "Those who have had a bath need only to wash their feet; their whole body is clean. And you are clean, though not every one of you." For he knew who was going to betray him, and that was why he said not everyone was clean. When he had finished washing their feet, he put on his clothes and returned to his place. "Do you understand what I have done for you?" he asked them. "You call me 'Teacher' and 'Lord,' and rightly so, for that is what I am. Now that I, your Lord and Teacher, have washed your feet, you also should wash one another's feet. I have set you an example that you should do as I have done for you. Very truly I tell you, no servant is greater than his master, nor is a messenger greater than the one who sent him. Now that you know these things, you will be blessed if you do them."

Jesus washes the feet of his followers, which was properly the responsibility of the house-servant (Fleming).

Examination of this passage shows that:

- o Jesus' basic motivation was love for his followers (v. 1).

- o Jesus was fully aware of his position as leader (v. 14).

- o Before the disciples experienced him as their servant, they had already experienced him many times before as Master, and as a strong and extremely powerful leader. Jesus voluntarily becomes a servant to his followers (v. 5-12).

- o He did not come primarily as their foot washer, but he was ready to do this service for his followers if needed.

- o Jesus wants to set an example for his followers to follow (v. 14-15).

JESUS SERVED HUMBLY

Jesus showed us how to serve; He wants us to be willing to serve Him in any way that glorifies God. John 13:4-5 says, "so he got up from the meal, took off his outer clothing, and wrapped a towel around his waist. After that, he poured water into a basin and began to wash his disciples' feet, drying them with the towel that was wrapped around him."

Are we willing to humble our self and serve as a leader? Even serve those who are overlooked, needy or outcasts in our society?

To serve without needing any affirmation, feedback or praise might be difficult for you.

JESUS SERVED OBEDIENTLY

Following Jesus' example, we must serve Him obediently and lovingly. "When he had finished washing their feet, he put on his clothes and returned to his place. "Do you understand what I have done for you?" he asked them. "You call me Teacher and Lord and rightly so, for that is what I am. Now that I, your Lord and Teacher have washed your feet, you should also wash one another's feet...Now that you know these things, you will be blessed if you do them" (John 13:12-16).

CHARACTERISTICS OF JESUS AS A SERVANT

Jesus Christ laid aside his Majesty to come to earth to show us the love of God. This action shows the characteristics of Jesus as a servant-leader. There is no doubt that when Christ came to earth, he also revealed his skills as a leader. His example as a servant, however, cannot be ignored.

Jesus' ministry has a strong foundation in servanthood. On one occasion, he told his disciples:

> "My command is this: Love each other as I have loved you. Greater love has no one than this: to lay down one's life for one's friends" (John 15:12-13).

These are the words of a true servant. Christ's life and death on the cross are the supreme example of his commitment to be a servant. There are several passages of scripture within the Bible that define the servant role of Jesus.

Isaiah describes the Messiah (Jesus) as a Servant. The Old Testament prophet Isaiah speaks of the coming "Messiah" as a servant. In his writing, the prophet points out the characteristics of a servant-leader. Jesus Christ came into this world as God's servant (Isaiah 42:1; 52:13; Acts 3:26; 4:27).

Isaiah wrote:

> "Here is my servant, whom I uphold, my chosen one in whom I delight; I will put my Spirit on him, and he will bring justice to the nations. He will not shout or cry out or raise his voice in the streets. A bruised reed he will not break, and a smouldering wick he will not snuff out. In faithfulness he will bring forth justice; he will not falter or be discouraged till he establishes

justice on earth. In his teaching the islands will put their hope" (Isaiah 42:1-4).

"See, my servant will act wisely; he will be raised and lifted up and highly exalted" (Isaiah 52:13).

He also came to serve man:

"Just as the Son of Man did not come to be served, but to serve, and to give his life as a ransom for many." (Matthew 20:28).

However, Christ did not come to be our servant, whereas he came out of obedience to God, serving him. Christians are called to be God's servants in every aspect of their lives. From the Bible it's clear that this means serving fellow man in accordance with the higher purpose of serving God. Note however, that simply serving people is insufficient. It does not necessarily imply that a leader is serving God. It is possible, for instance, to serve people based on a humanistic worldview. There is a big difference between serving the needs of others and being a servant of others' needs.

The servant leader is a growing leader, led and grown by the Holy Spirit. These factors are necessary to help the leader apply power in line with God's purpose and for the best of the followers. The development and growth of Three-dimension Servant Leaders.

There are three dimensions in which Christian servant leaders must grow:

a. As a voluntary servant of God

b. As a servant of others, and

c. As a leader.

If someone is already a committed servant of God and of others, they need to employ their leadership gifts to serve others as a leader with the right use of power and love. Leadership skills training, continuous encouragement and feedback can support a servant leader in this growth process.

Someone, who is already a leader, but who wants to become a servant leader, also needs training, encouragement and feedback, but they have a greater need for conversion towards servanthood. This commitment must then be strengthened again and again. It is harder to learn to be a servant than to learn to be a leader, especially for those who have been senior leaders for many years. Old habits die hard (Grahn).

The servant leader must be a 'learning servant' who wants to grow both as a leader and as a servant. Therefore, the servant leader invites feedback especially from God – through prayer, Bible reading, and communication with spiritual mentors and the people being served. One way to start a feedback process with the people being served is simply to ask them how the leader can best serve them. Ideally the feedback will be an ongoing process, resulting in the servant leader serving more effectively according to the actual needs of the people.

According to the Bible, to become a servant of God and to enjoy serving others is not only a decision that a person needs to take, but first a gracious gift from God. More than this, because of our new nature, as Christian leaders we should find ourselves readily drawn to the Christ-centred servant leadership model. It is the leadership style of our role model, Jesus Christ, and as we see throughout the Bible, serving God inherently includes serving others in line with his good plans and purposes.

Matthew 20:28 says, "... just as the Son of Man did not come to be served, but to serve and to give his life as a ransom for many." He came to teach, lead and train. How did He do this? He served. Jesus' mandate is for us to make disciples, teaching them to obey everything that He taught.

Jesus was born to give His life. From early beginnings, He stayed in step with his Father's plans. He knew and accepted his calling, kept it as the central focus, even in the formative years. Remember early on in his life and three-day disappearance?

His anxious and stressed-out parents finally found him in the courtyard of the temple, listening and asking the synagogue teachers questions. Although Mary and Joseph were relieved, they became irritated and offended over his behaviour. We find Jesus' response in Luke 2:49, "Why were you searching for me? Didn't you know I had to be in my Father's house?" Jesus was born to give his life. Jesus was born to serve. He showed us how to serve those in his inner circle; his twelve disciples. As He prepared himself for the cross in the upper room at the last supper, surrounded by those he loved, he readied them for his death. John 13:1 says, "Having loved his own who were in the world, he now showed them the full extent of his love."

JESUS SERVED LOVINGLY

What did He do to show his love? He served his men in a humble way, by washing the disciples' feet. This was taking the place of a servant in its lowest form. At the Last Supper, Jesus would have been the 'host' and the apostles the 'guests'. Washing the feet of weary travellers would have been a job assigned to a gentile slave by the host. Not even a Jewish slave would be expected to do this lowly job as a servant. The host of a meal would never lower himself to performing this vile task himself. The travellers in ancient Palestine would have worn sandals; their feet would have been filthy from traveling on dirt roads. "Christ Jesus, though he was in the form of God, did not count equality with God a thing to be grasped, but emptied himself, taking the form of a servant" (Phil. 2:5-7).

What would you do if you thought your death was imminent, or like Jesus, die by execution? Jesus chose to lovingly serve. Is Jesus asking you to show your love to him in a way you hadn't planned? You say, wait a minute, that's not the way I thought it would be. Yet God says, this is right where I want you. How might God be asking you to serve him? That is how you will show your love to him, by your loving and committed obedience.

JESUS DESCRIBES HIMSELF AS A SERVANT IN HIS TEACHING

In three of the Gospels, Jesus refers to himself and his ministry in the world. In those three passages of scripture, Christ lays out the characteristics of true servanthood:

> "For even the Son of Man did not come to be served, but to serve, and to give his life as a ransom for many" Mark 10:45 (NIV).

> "For I have come down from heaven not to do my will but to do the will of him who sent me" John 6:38 (NIV).

> "For who is greater, the one who is at the table or the one who serves? Is it not the one who is at the table? But I am among you as one who serves" Luke 22:27 (NIV).

Jesus points out in these three scriptures basic truths about servanthood:

- A true servant does not seek to be served.
- A true servant aims to serve others.
- A true servant does not aim to do his own will.
- A true servant does not promote himself.
- Jesus Shows Himself as a Servant by His Actions

The idea of being a servant is not always accepted by those around us. Simon Peter had a very difficult time in allowing Jesus to wash his feet. This action was the role of the 'servant'. Jesus made it clear to Simon that this was the foundation of all that he had been teaching the disciples.

THE APOSTLE PAUL DESCRIBES JESUS AS A SERVANT

In his letter to the first-century church at Philippi, the Apostle Paul had this to say about the servant role of Jesus:

> "Who, being in very nature God, did not consider equality with God something to be used to his own advantage; rather, he made himself nothing by taking the very nature of a servant, being made in human likeness" Philippians 2:6-7 (NIV).

Paul also taught the early Christian believers that servanthood and humility work together. He wrote about the example that Jesus sets:

> "And being found in appearance as a man, he humbled himself by becoming obedient to death—even death on a cross!" Philippians 2:8 (NIV).

Paul points out to the believers that Christ's example of servanthood is one of the most powerful messages of the New Testament church.

Jesus was not a self-promoting servant; he had several opportunities to promote himself, but he never did. The Gospel of Matthew tell a story of how Jesus had every opportunity to promote himself but refused to do it. One of those stories can be seen here:

> "Departing from there, He went into their synagogue. And a man was there whose hand was withered. And they questioned Jesus, asking, "Is it lawful to heal on the Sabbath?"—so that they might accuse Him. And He said to them, "What man is there among you who has a sheep, and if it falls into a pit on the Sabbath, will he not take hold of it and lift it out? How much more valuable, then, is a man than a sheep! So then, it is lawful to do good on the

Sabbath." Then He said to the man, "Stretch out your hand!" He stretched it out, and it was restored to normal, like the other. But the Pharisees went out and conspired against Him, as to how they might destroy Him. But Jesus, aware of this, withdrew from there. Many followed Him, and He healed them all, and warned them not to tell who He was. This was to fulfil what was spoken through Isaiah the prophet: "Behold, My Servant whom I have chosen; My Beloved in whom My soul is well-pleased; I will put My Spirit upon Him, And He shall proclaim justice to the Gentiles. "He will not quarrel, nor cry out; Nor will anyone hear His voice in the streets. "A battered reed He will not break off, and a smouldering wick He will not put out, Until He leads justice to victory. And in His name the Gentiles will hope" (Matthew 12:9-21).

Jesus, as a servant-leader, taught that humility and servanthood cannot be separated, he said to his disciples in the Gospel of Matthew.

"But when you give to the needy, do not let your left hand know what your right hand is doing, so that your giving may be in secret. Then your Father, who sees what is done in secret, will reward you" (Matthew 6:3-4NIV).

JESUS PRAISES THE CHARACTER OF A TRUSTING SERVANT

Real and powerful servanthood starts by recognizing the power of others. A centurion soldier came to Jesus asking for help.

Matthew records the story:

"When Jesus had entered Capernaum, a centurion came to him, asking for help. "Lord," he said, "my servant lies at home paralysed, suffering terribly." Jesus said to him, "Shall I come and heal him?" The centurion replied, "Lord, I do not deserve to have you come under my

> roof. But just say the word, and my servant will be healed. For I myself am a man under authority, with soldiers under me. I tell this one, 'Go,' and he goes; and that one, 'Come,' and he comes. I say to my servant, 'Do this,' and he does it." When Jesus heard this, he was amazed and said to those following him, "Truly I tell you, I have not found anyone in Israel with such great faith" (Matthew 8:5-10).

This story has a significant meaning. Here is a soldier who has authority and power at his fingertips; yet he placed himself under the authority of Jesus. This encounter with the soldier impressed Jesus. This man was willing to place himself under the authority and leadership of Jesus much like a servant. This centurion is a perfect example of humble servanthood. Jesus even said, "Truly I tell you; I have not found anyone in Israel with such great faith.". Jesus as a servant leader is a powerful example to follow.

When thinking about the servant style of Jesus it would benefit any leader to follow his example.
John Stott put it this way:

> "The authority by which the Christian leader leads is not power but love, not force but example, not coercion but reasoned persuasion. Leaders have power, but power is safe only in the hands of those who humble themselves to serve" (Runn).

This is exactly the example that Jesus set for those who are willing to follow Him. The teachings and lifestyle of Jesus are significant in the Christian's life. He is the essential role model for how we seek to live out our lives. It's interesting, therefore, that his model is often sadly neglected when it comes to aspects of church and organisational leadership. He was the prototype of Christian leadership.

'The King Who Led with a Towel' is a three-part article that examines Jesus' leadership style and example. It is extracted from culture craft by Rick Sessoms and Colin Buckland and Rick's original 2003 paper. Their dialogue introduces us to the explicit leadership lessons that Jesus gave to his Disciples and his leadership values. They provide key insights into a practical and effective style of leadership for Christian leaders in both churches and other organisations.

This first part of 'The King Who Led with a Towel' considers the lessons that Jesus taught his Disciples about leadership and part two looks at the servant leadership values that Jesus demonstrated.

A DIFFERENT LEADERSHIP STYLE

The time was Passover, the most sacred of Jewish feasts. Three million people would have been in Jerusalem for this celebration week. Word had spread like wildfire through the city that Jesus of Nazareth was on his way to the feast. Thousands lined the road as Jesus made his way into Jerusalem. "Hosanna!" they chanted. "Blessed is he who comes in the name of the Lord. Blessed is the kingdom of our father David!" But Jesus wasn't what the crowd expected. They expected a conquering King. He disappointed the Passover pilgrims that week. And in so doing, he fulfilled their most profound needs. This is made graphically clear a few days later when Jesus and his friends had gathered for a meal. Since the streets and roads of Palestine were plain dirt – in dry weather they were deep in dust, and in wet weather they could become liquid mud – the shoes people wore in that day were simple: a flat sole, held onto the feet by a few straps. So, every walk in the street soiled the feet. That's why just inside the doorway of homes sat a basin of water with a towel. The custom was for a servant to greet visitors and wash their feet.

But on this night when Jesus gathered his disciples for a meal, the wash basin sat unused. Of course, the disciples had their minds riveted on more noble thoughts. The talk of the week had ignited their imaginations of the Kingdom of God - dreams of thrones and power and glory. In fact, they were conflicted about which of them would be the greatest in this Kingdom, while everybody in the house had dirty feet. So, Jesus got up from the table, prepared himself, and started to wash the feet of his followers. Here is the King of Kings, washing filthy feet, and drying them with a towel. Here is a King whose symbol of authority is a towel. Jesus demonstrated and taught three lessons about leadership in his use of the towel that night.

Lesson 1: Jesus' use of the 'towel' represented His whole life and leadership.

The first lesson is that the towel dramatises not only Jesus' leadership, but also his whole life. Washing his Disciples' feet was no isolated event. On the contrary, what Jesus did that night in the upper room vividly portrays the whole journey He made from the Father into the world and back to the Father. Jesus laid aside His garments that night just as he had laid aside His glory in heaven and his privileges as the Son of God. He washed men's feet, a lowly act of service, just as He died the degrading death of a common criminal. When Jesus had finished washing their feet, he took up his garments and returned to his place of honour, just as he was taken up from the grave and seated again with God the Father.

In this upper room, the Son of Man stripped off His garments, got down on his knees, and washed dirt from the feet of those whom He had called to follow Him as a fitting symbol of His whole life and leadership.

Lesson 2: Jesus' use of the 'towel' revealed His perspective on positional power.

The second lesson is that the towel revealed Jesus' own concept of positional power. From a human perspective, washing feet is beneath the dignity of a King. In fact, Peter reflected his shock at Jesus' actions when he responded, "you shall never wash my feet". Peter wanted Jesus to fit into human ideas of royalty and privilege. In this foot-washing, Jesus dismantled our concept of position and pecking order. We live with the notion that to be leader is to be exalted, but in his use of the towel, Jesus revealed that being God means coming down from his throne and giving himself to serve.

Peter would have been perfectly comfortable washing Jesus' feet. That would be normal according to human ideas. But to see Jesus – the great I AM – stoop before Peter and begin to reach for his dirty feet is not normal. Just before coming into Jerusalem that week, Jesus told his Disciples, "for even the Son of Man came not to be served but to serve and give his life a ransom for many." In that one line He turned everything upside down.

Lesson 3: Jesus' use of the 'towel' teaches us to serve God by serving others.

After washing their feet, Jesus said to His Disciples: "Do you understand what I have done for you? You call me 'Teacher' and 'Lord', and rightly so, for that is what I am. Now that I, your Lord and Teacher, have washed your feet, you should wash one another's feet."

What a profound statement! If Jesus had said "Now that I've washed your feet, you wash my feet", we would be standing in line for the privilege of being first with the towel and the basin to wash God's feet. But Jesus said, "Now that I have washed your feet, you wash one another's feet." We are a debtor to Jesus the King for what he has paid for us.

WHAT LEADING WITH THE TOWEL MEANS

Leading with the 'towel' means believing in people enough to empower them with the authority, resources, information and accountability they need to be the best they can be. It means creating an environment safe enough for them to risk giving all and sometimes fail in their giving, and encouraging them to risk again. Leading with the 'towel' implies that I don't have to be the source of every good idea, because we discover the vision together. It is all about creating an atmosphere where everyone is free to tell the truth, especially to the leaders. Leading with the 'towel' means allowing people to express their passion. It means defending those who don't compromise principle for profit both publicly and privately. It also means treating each person with the sacred understanding that they are uniquely crafted in the image of their Creator, not in mine. Leading with the 'towel' is enabling people to make decisions and pursue their God given dreams, celebrating their accomplishments. Leading with the 'towel' means serving those I lead not so that they will serve me, but so that they will serve others.

But as leaders we need to admit, there is a tension within us as we considered these things. As a leader, this way of relating to people is not normal. It's often not the way we have related to people in the past. This way of relating to people reverses the order; it is subversive. It destabilises. But, isn't that precisely what Jesus intends? I think we're beginning to grasp the Gospel of the Kingdom. Jesus changes our whole concept of power, authority and status. When the Disciples were arguing about who would be greatest, He said to them, "you know that those who are recognised as rulers of the Gentiles lord it over them … But it is not so among you. Whoever wishes to become great among you shall be your servant, and whoever wishes to be number one shall be slave to all. For even the Son of Man did not come to be served but to serve" (Matthew 20:25-28).

The King who led with a towel inaugurated a kingdom of foot washers. He deleted the icon of leaders clamouring for power, people climbing over each other to get to the top. Jesus' example even puts to rest the notion that I wash your feet so that you wash mine. Rather, I wash your feet so that you can, in turn, wash another's feet. That which distinguishes Jesus' way of leadership is brought into being by the self-emptying love of Jesus Himself. When leaders belong to King Jesus, we can no longer write on our resume, "I don't wash feet." That's precisely what leaders do because that's what Jesus does.

As liberating as it is, this way of leadership doesn't just happen. As much as we may want to be this kind of leader, often we find our self-expressing with the Apostle Paul, "Lord, what I do is not the good I want to do, and the evil I do not want to do – this I keep on doing... who will rescue me?" (Romans 7:19-24).

Many times, we are unable to lead this way – at least with any consistency. In those times, when we are unable, or unwilling, to take up the 'towel'; when we find our self in that place where Jesus' way of leadership just doesn't make sense, it usually means that it's time to let Him wash our feet again. It's time to let this King who knew where he had come from and where he was going, this King who knew that He was in the absolute centre of his Father's will, this King whose heart is overflowing with love, to wash our feet again. For to the degree that we allow him to love and serve us, we can wash the feet of those we lead into the liberty of the Kingdom of God.

This part looks at the different leadership values he exhibited and the third part, "Applying the Towel" will outline the framework that underpins its practical application.

JESUS DIFFERENT LEADERSHIP VALUES

There is so much more biblical insight into Jesus' life and leadership that will have to wait for a more complete revelation. For now, let's look at the practical implications. What does it mean to lead with these principles of Jesus to craft a healthier organisation?

We don't want to imply that there is a simple answer, but we can begin by looking at three cardinal values that shaped Jesus' leadership.

Value 1: Jesus; leadership was established upon a relationship with his followers.

From Genesis to Revelation is described a God who desires a relationship with the people He created. Restored relationship with God is central to the Gospel message. In the same theme, leadership for Jesus existed in the context of relationship with His followers. Regarding the importance of relationship in leadership, the account in Luke when Jesus inspired Simon Peter to leave his nets and fish for men. In order to lead Simon, Jesus entered Simon's world (the fishing boat), met his need (catching fish), and spoke to him with dignity (invited him to a higher calling). In these practical ways, Jesus summoned Simon to follow Him through relationship. In other Gospel accounts, we read that Jesus invested time eating, socialising and travelling with his Disciples and others. Other examples from Jesus' leadership that demonstrated his commitment to relationships with followers are:

- His vulnerability in the Garden to His three friends when He was facing Gethsemane.
- His patient explanation of parables to the Disciples.
- His statement to his Disciples: "You are my friends."
- His encounter with the Samaritan woman when He engaged her in conversation and communicated His concern and care for her as a person.
- His healing of Jairus' daughter.

From these biblical examples and many others, we can conclude that many people chose to follow Jesus because of His relationship with them.

Through the Bible, God led people through a relationship with those who chose to follow Him.

Value 2: Jesus' leadership was activated by influence, not coercive power.

Jesus demonstrated that leadership is activated by influence, not by manipulation. Jesus held no positional power over those he was leading. They had a choice to follow Him or to turn away and reject His invitation. Therefore, God's creation of human will; our freedom to choose, was one of God's most profound acts of authentic leadership. The fact that Jesus came as a baby of low socioeconomic status implies a God who leads not based on power, but through influencing His willing followers.

The Gospels are filled with examples of Jesus' incredible personal and spiritual influence with his Disciples and many others, including those who disagreed with Him and those who ultimately crucified Him.

Some examples include:
- Multitudes came to hear him speak on many occasions.
- Simon dropped everything and followed Him.
- Large crowds followed him.
- Jesus' encounter with His accusers on the morning of the Crucifixion.
- Jesus' conversation with the thief on the cross.

People who had the free choice followed Jesus because of His massive personal and spiritual influence.

So, what are implications of this principle? The capacity to influence others is the characteristic that primarily distinguishes leaders from followers. The true leaders in an organisation are not necessarily those people who are appointed by the board. Authentic leadership by influence is not subject to organisational charts; the real leaders in any organisation influence both those 'above' and 'below' them on the organisational chart.

One way to determine whether one is a leader is to evaluate whether others are following because they want to (free will) or because they must. Unfortunately, many Christian organisations make the mistake of appointing people as the spiritual leaders rather than affirming those who are already recognised as the spiritual leaders. This is often a tragic misstep for the welfare of the organisation since these appointed individuals establish the spiritual climate into the organisation's future.

Value 3: Jesus prioritised His followers' potential over His own benefit.

The value that really set apart Jesus' way of leadership from all other leadership approaches was His priority on the followers' potential. Jesus' leadership was focused on his Followers' Kingdom potential, not on His well-being or the benefit of any religious organisation that He was building. This principle seems to be very controversial since leaders are usually appointed to build a successful organisation.

That's right. All leaders desire to be successful, or at least 'fruitful'. After all, how will the organisation be successful unless the leader is successful? This third value is radical. Jesus did not invest His life in others to build a successful organisation. Jesus invested His life in others so that they could grow to their maximum Kingdom potential.

This type of leadership is risky, but it stands at the heart of Jesus' way of leadership. The religious establishment in Jesus' day was building a system that seemed infinitely stronger and more permanent than what Jesus was doing. But He was building people to be their very best. The church was a by-product of Jesus' primary focus during His three years of ministry. He developed eleven followers who were transformed to reach their highest potential.

If the weight of the Gospel writings is any indication of where Jesus spent his time and energy, Jesus evidently spent almost no time investing in a religious system. In fact, He consistently challenged the religious system and its leaders. Rather, most of Jesus' time was spent teaching and preaching with the goal of transforming lives and reproducing his heart for the world into those who would carry the torch after his departure. On the night before His crucifixion, Jesus foretold the coming of the Holy Spirit who would lead them to do even greater things than they had heretofore experienced. In his appearance to them just before his ascension, Jesus exhorted his Disciples to be empowered by the Spirit and be witnesses. These priorities demonstrate a deep commitment for his Disciples to reach their highest Kingdom potential. The church's early momentum and sustained perpetuity for twenty-one centuries was birthed through Jesus' sacrificial resolve to lead by focusing on his followers' highest potential.

As this is true, it distinguishes Jesus' leadership from so many utilitarian leadership models that are discarded if they aren't successful. Those who lead Jesus' way do so not because it is the most successful way to lead, but because it is the right way to lead.

Leadership is not telling people what to do but living out yourself what you want those you influence to embody.

On the night that Jesus was betrayed, his Disciples argued over who would have the greatest title among them; "and he said to them, "The kings of the Gentiles exercise lordship over them, and those in authority over them are called benefactors. But not so with you. Rather, let the greatest among you become as the youngest, and the leader as one who serves. For who is the greater, one who reclines at table or one who serves? Is it not the one who reclines at table? But I am among you as the one who serves" (Luke 22:24–27 ESV).

The Disciples wanted a title, and Jesus gave them a towel! Shockingly, Jesus––the Son of God, the King of Kings, the

Great I Am––washed the feet of his disciples to embody the kind of leaders he wanted them to become.

"Jesus, knowing that the Father had given all things into his hands, and that he had come from God and was going back to God, rose from supper. He laid aside his outer garments, and taking a towel, tied it around his waist. Then he poured water into a basin and began to wash the Disciples' feet and to wipe them with the towel that was wrapped around him" (John 13:3–5).

This is the essence of leadership: beauty and power. Imagine how different the world would be if we led this way?

HOW WAS JESUS ABLE TO HUMBLE HIMSELF?

Ken Boa in Conformed to His Image shares an insight into why Jesus, in his humanity, was able to humble himself:

- o He knew where his dignity and power came from ("knowing that the Father had given all things into his hands").
- o He knew his significance and identity ("and that he had come from God").
- o He knew his security and destiny ("and was going back to God").

When God's people know that their dignity, power, significance, identity, security, and destiny are rooted in the limitless, unconditional love of God in Christ, we, too, can ask for a towel, instead of a title. Just about that (Boa 44).

All professing Christians agree that a Christian leader should be a servant leader. Jesus could not be clearer:

"The kings of the Gentiles exercise lordship over them, and those in authority over them are called benefactors. But not so with you. Rather, let the greatest among you become as the youngest, and the leader as one who serves." (Luke 22:25–26)

There is not always agreement is how servant leadership should look in each situation. Sometimes servant leaders wash others' feet, so to speak (John 13:1–17), but other times they rebuke (Matthew 16:23), and even discipline (Matthew 18:15–20). Sometimes they serve at their own expense (1 Corinthians 9:7), but other times they issue strong imperatives (1 Corinthians 5:2; 11:16).

"A servant leader sacrificially seeks the highest joy of those he serves." So, determining whether a leader is acting from a heart of Christlike service requires charitable, patient, and humble discernment. It's not that simple. There's no one-size-fits-all servant leader description. The needs and contexts in the wider church are vast and varied and require many kinds of leaders and gifts. We must guard against our own unique biases when assessing leaders' hearts. Each of us is drawn to certain kinds of leaders, but our preferences can be unreliable and even uncharitable standards marks of a Servant Leader. Still, the New Testament instructs us to exercise due diligence in discerning a Christian leader's fitness (1 Timothy 3:1–13). What traits do we look for in a leader that suggests his fundamental orientation is Christlike servanthood? This list is by no means exhaustive, but here are five fundamental indicators:

1. A servant leader seeks the glory of his Master.

The reputation is not his master neither his ministry constituency; it is God. Jesus said, "the one who speaks on his own authority seeks his own glory; but the one who seeks the glory of him who sent him is true, and in him there is no falsehood" (John 7:18). A Christlike leader is a bondservant of Christ (Ephesians 6:6) and demonstrates over time that Christ - not public approval, position, or financial security - has his primary loyalty. In this he "swears to his own hurt and does not change" (Psalm 15:4).

2. A servant leader sacrificially seeks the highest joy of those he serves.

This does not conflict with seeking the glory of his Master. Jesus said, "whoever would be great among you must be your servant . . . even as the Son of Man came not to be served but to serve, and to give his life as a ransom for many" (Matthew 20:26, 28). Whatever his temperament, gift mix, capacities, or sphere of influence, he will make necessary sacrifices in order to pursue people's "progress and joy in the faith," which results in the greater glory of God (Philippians 1:25; 2:9–11).

3. A servant leader will sacrifice his rights rather than obscure the gospel.

> "A servant leader's identity and trust are not in his calling, but in his Christ."

Paul said it this way: "I have made myself a servant to all, that I might win more of them" (1 Corinthians 9:19). What did this mean for him? It meant sometimes he abstained from certain foods and drinks, or refused financial support from those he served, or worked with his own hands to provide for himself, or went hungry, or dressed poorly, or was beaten, or was homeless, or endured disrespect inside and outside the church (1 Corinthians 4:11–13; 9:4–7). He also decided not to marry (1 Corinthians 9:5). This all before he was martyred. Paul's servant bar may have been set extraordinarily high, but all servant leaders will yield their rights if they believe more will be won to Christ as a result.

4. A servant leader is not preoccupied with personal visibility and recognition.

Like John the Baptist, a servant leader sees himself as a "friend of the Bridegroom" (John 3:29) and is not preoccupied with the visibility of his own role. He doesn't view those with less visible roles as less significant, nor does he covet more visible roles as more significant (1 Corinthians 12:12–26). He seeks to steward the role he's received as best he can and gladly leaves the role assignments to God (John 3:27).

5. A servant leader anticipates and graciously accepts the time for his decrease.

All leaders serve only for a season. Some seasons are long, some short; some are abundant, some lean; some are recorded and recalled, most are not. But all seasons end. When John the Baptist recognised the ending of his season, he said, "therefore this joy of mine is now complete. He must increase, but I must decrease" (John 3:29–30). Sometimes a leader is the first to recognise his season's end, sometimes others recognise it first, and sometimes God lets a season end unjustly for purposes a leader cannot understand at the time. A servant leader graciously yields his role for the good of Christ's cause, because his identity and trust are not in his calling, but in his Christ.

Therefore, we need to be Gracious with our Leaders because no earthly Christian leader is the perfect incarnation of these five fundamental marks of servanthood. Jesus alone bears that distinction. Most of our leaders are imperfect servants trying to be faithful.

That why we need to give and to show love to our leaders:

a. our explicit encouragement when we see any of these graces in them (loose our tongues),

b. our quiet patience with their stumbling (hold our tongues), and

c. our charitable judgment and gracious feedback regarding decisions that raise questions and concerns (bridle our tongues).

All three can be as easily applied in speaking about our leaders as in speaking to them. (McBean)

The 20th century was blessed by a woman who epitomised servant leadership. Theresa Bojaxhiu was born and raised in Albania. For years, she washed the feet, hands, heads, and bodies of the poorest in Calcutta and Manila and other cities. But she also touched those who are not poor. One such man was Malcolm Muggeridge, formerly a prominent broadcaster with the BBC. So, touched was Muggeridge by her that he wrote a book in her honour, entitled Something Beautiful for God (Muggeridge).

In that book, he wrote these words: "To choose as Mother Teresa did to live in the slums of Calcutta amidst all the dirt and disease and misery signified a spirit so indomitable, a faith so intractable, a love so abounding that I felt abashed." Muggeridge went on to tell of an experience he had in Calcutta to which he responded by retreating to his comfortable hotel room and complaining about the wretched condition of the city. Then he wrote these words: "I ran away and stayed away. But Mother Teresa moved in and stayed. That was the difference. She, a slightly built nun, few rubbles in her pocket, not particularly clever or gifted in the art of persuasion, came with Christian love shining about her."

The life of Mother Theresa reflected to the modern world a similar model that Jesus taught his disciples with the towel. The towel dramatised Jesus' whole life. The towel revealed the nature of his leadership. His use of the towel is an example for leaders everywhere. Families, organisations and societies in all cultures around the world will be healthier when leaders follow Jesus' example daily.

CONCLUSION

So much of what we read in Christian circles on leadership is about 'how to lead' instead of 'how to embody what you want those you influence to become'. I believe leadership is not telling people what to do but living out yourself what you want those you influence to embody.

On the night that Jesus was betrayed, his Disciples argued over who would have the greatest title among them, "And he said to them, the Kings of the Gentiles exercise lordship over them, and those in authority over them are called benefactors. But not so with you. Rather, let the greatest among you become as the youngest, and the leader as one who serves. For who is the greater, one who reclines at table or one who serves? Is it not the one who reclines at table? But I am among you as the one who serves." (Luke 22:24–27)

The servant leader sacrificially seeks the highest joy of those he serves. This does not conflict with seeking the glory of his Master. Jesus said, "Whoever would be great among you must be your servant . . . even as the Son of Man came not to be served but to serve, and to give his life as a ransom for many" (Matthew 20:26, 28). Whatever his temperament, gift mix, capacities, or sphere of influence, he will make necessary sacrifices in order to pursue people's "progress and joy in the faith," which results in the greater glory of God.

A servant leader will sacrifice his rights rather than obscure the gospel, a servant leader's identity and trust are not in his calling, title or position, but in Christ. He involves a mature worldview that chooses service over self-interest like Jesus who submitted his own life to sacrificial service under the will of God Although he was God's son and was thus more powerful than any other leader in the world, laying aside his Majesty to come to earth to show us the love of God. This action shows the characteristics of Jesus as a servant-leader. There is no doubt that when Christ came to earth, he also revealed his skills as a leader, however; his example as a servant cannot be ignored. Jesus was born to give His life. From early beginnings, He stayed in step with His Father's plans. He knew and accepted His calling, kept it as the central focus, even in the formative years. When thinking about the servant style of Jesus it would benefit any leader to follow his example.

The authority by which the Christian leader leads is not power but love, not force but example, not coercion but reasoned persuasion. Leaders have power, but power is safe only in the hands of those who humble themselves to serve. This is exactly the example that Jesus set for those who are willing to follow Him.

The teachings and lifestyle of Jesus are significant in the Christian's life. He is the essential role model for how we seek to live out our lives. It's interesting, therefore, that his model is often sadly neglected when it comes to aspects of church and organisational leadership. He was the prototype of Christian leadership.

Men and women in search of excellence in developing their leadership abilities will find much to aid their quest in this close look at Jesus the greatest leader who ever lived. The more we understand the Bible, the more evident it becomes that everything about effective leadership Jesus did to perfection. He is simply the greatest leadership role model of all time.

BIBLIOGRAPHY

Armour, Michael, Browning, Don. *Systems-Sensitive Leadership*: Empowering Diversity Without Polarizing the Church. Missouri: College Pres Publishing, 2000. Print

AZaleznik, Abraham. "Managers and Leaders: Are They Different?" *Harvard Business Review*. Web. Jan 2004. <https://hbr.org/2004/01/managers-and-leaders-are-they-different>

Barker, Joel. *Paradigms*. The Business of Discovering the Future. New York: Harper Collins Publishers, 1992. Print.

Barrett, Colleen. "What Is Servant Leadership?" *Thoughts from Southwest Airlines President, Colleen Barrett*. Web. 20 Sept. 2010. < https://www.quickbase.com/.../what-is-servant-leadership-thoughts-from-southwest-air>

Bartle, Christian. "Worldview of Leadership." Web. 26 Sept. 2012 <https://www.bartleby.com/.../Christian-Worldview-of-Leadership-PKRSYC343RYYA>

Bass, Jossey. *The Jossey-Bass Reader on Educational Leadership*. San Francisco: John Wiley & Son, Inc, 2007. Print

Block, Peter. *Stewardship*: Choosing Service Over Self-Interest. San Francisco: Berrett-Koehler Publishers, 1993. Print

Boa, Kenneth. *Conformed to His Image*: Biblical and Practical Approaches to Spiritual Formation. Grand Rapids: Zondervan, 2001. Print.

Bolden, Richard., Jonathan, Gosling, Antonio and Marturano, P.Dennison. "A Review of Leadership Theory and Competency Frameworks." *Centre for Leadership Studies*. Web. June 2013. <https://www.researchgate.net/.../29810623_A_Review_of_Leadership_Theory_and_C>

Bradberry, Travis. "What Really Makes a Good Leader?" Entrepreneur. Web. 14 Sept. 2015 <https://www.entrepreneur.com/article/249905>

Chao, Peter. "Leading with Courage." 5 Dec. Web. 5Dec. 2013

< www.leadership.com.sg/perspective/worldview/leading-with-courage/>

Chao, Peter. "Leading from Being." *Insight, Ideas and Inspiration for The Leaders*. Web. 5 Sept. 2014. <www.leadership.com.sg/perspective/worldview/leading-from-being/>

Covey, Stephen R. *The 7 Habits of Highly Effective People*: Restoring the Character Ethic. New York: Simon & Schuster, 1989. Print.

Daft, Richard, Robert H. Lengel. *Fusion Leadership:* Unlocking the Subtle Forces that Change People and Organisations. San Francisco: Berret-Koehler, Inc, 1998. Print

De Bono, Silvio, Joop Remme, Stephanie Jones, Beatrice van der Heijden. *Leadership, Change and Responsibility*. Oxford: Meyer & Meyer Media, 2008. Print

DePree, Max. "Leadership." *Leading from Being*. Web. 5 Sept. 2014 <www.leadership.com.sg/perspective/worldview/leading-from-being>

Dierendonck, V. Dirk. "Servant Leadership." *A Review and Synthesis*. Web. 2 Sept. 2010. <journals.sagepub.com/doi/10.1177/0149206310380462 >

Fleming, Walter. "The Religious and Hospitable Rite of Feet Washing" *Johns Hopkins University Press*. Vol. 16, No. 1, 1908.

Fiedler, Fred. "A Contingency Model of Leadership Effectiveness." Web. 10 Apr. 2008. "FE Fiedler - Advances in experimental social psychology, 1964 – Elsevier"

Grahn, Thorsten. "Jesus: The Role Model for Christian Leadership." *Leadership Style, Modeled on Jesus, Servant Leadership.* Web. 08 Nov. 2011. <christian-leadership.org/jesus-the-role-model-for-christian-leaders>

Greenleaf, Robert K. *Servant Leadership*: A Journey into the Nature of Legitimate Power and Greatness. New York: Paulist Press, 1977. Print

Greenleaf, Robert. *The Servant as Leader*: A Journey into the Nature of Legitimate Power and Greatness. New York: Paulist Press, 2002. Print

Hersey, Paul. "Management of organizational behaviour": *Leading Human Resources.* <PHersey, KH Blanchard, DE Johnson 2007>

Hersey, Paul, Kenneth H. Blanchard, Walter E. Natemeyer. "Situational Leadership, Perception, and the Impact of Power." Web. 1 Dec. <journals.sagepub.com/doi/10.1177/105960117900400404>

Hersey, Paul, Kenneth H. Blanchard. "Management of Organizational Behaviour." *Utilizing Human Resources*, 6th Edition. Englewood Cliffs, NJ: Prentice-Hall, 1993. Web.

Heylighen, Francis. "What is a World View." *Principia Cybernetica*. Web.

Hybels, Bill. "Vision." *Paint the Picture Passionately*. Web. 14 Nov. 2011. <https://www.followthegls.com/leadership/vision-paint-the-picture-passionately>

Johannsen, Murray. "Types of Leadership Styles." *Twelve Worth Knowing and Using.* Web. 29 Apr. 2018. <https://www.legacee.com/types-of-leadership-styles>

Katzenbach, Jon, Douglas K. Smith. "The Discipline of Teams". *Harvard Business Review.* Web. July-August. <https://hbr.org/2005/07/the-discipline-of-teams>

Kruse, Kevin. "What Is Leadership?" *Forbes.* Web. 9 Apr. 2013 <https://www.forbes.com/sites/kevinkruse/2013/04/09/what-is-leadership/>

Lewin, Kurt. "Leadership Styles". *Choosing the Right Approach for the Situation.* Web. 1930. < https://www.mindtools.com › Leadership Skills › Leadership Styles >

Liden, R.C., Wayne, S.J., Liao, C., & Meuser, J.D. (2014). "Servant leadership and serving culture. Influence on individual and unit performance." *Academy of Management Journal*, 57. Print

Maslow, Abraham. "Law of the instrument". Web. 1966. <https://en.wikipedia.org/wiki/Law_of_the_instrument >

Maxwell, John. *21 Irrefutable Laws of Leadership*. Nashville: Thomas Nelson 2007. Print.

Maxwell, John. *The 360 Degree Leader*. Developing Your Influence from Anywhere in The Organisation. Nashville: Thomas Nelson, 2005. Print.

McBean, Billy. "The 5 Characteristics of Great Leaders." Web. 24 Jan. <https://www.fastcompany.com/3004914/5-characteristics-great-leaders>

McGregor, Douglas. "The Human Side of Enterprise." *Annotated Edition*. Massachusetts: MIT School of Industrial Management, 1957. Print.

Muggeridge, Malcolm. *Something Beautiful for God*. San Francisco: Harper & Row, 1971. Print.

Murphy, Bill. "7 Things Great Leaders Always Do but Mere Managers Always Fear." Web. < https://www.inc.com/.../7-things-great-leaders-always-do-but-mere-managers-always-fea>

Neff J. Thomas, Paul B. Brown, James M. Citrin. "Lessons from the Top." *The Search for America's Best Business Leaders*. New York: Broadway Business 1999. Print.

Phillips, Gary, William E. Brown. *Making Sense of Your World*. Chicago: Moody Press, 1991.

Runn, Gary. "John Stott on Leadership." *Spiritual Leadership*. Web. 14 Feb. 2013. <garyrunn.com/2013/02/14/john-stott-on-leadership>

Sire, James. "The Universe Next Door": *A Basic Worldview Catalog*. 4th edition. InterVarsity Press, 2004, 17.

Scouller, James. "The Three Levels of Leadership: How to Develop Your Leadership Presence." *Knowhow and Skill. Management Books* 2000 (2011): 34-35. Print

Spears, Larry, editor. "Reflections on Leadership." How Robert K. Greenleaf's *Theory of Servant-Leadership Influenced Today's Top Management Thinkers*. New York: John Wiley & Sons, Inc., 1995. Web.

Stogdill, R.M. *Handbook of leadership*: A survey of the literature. New York: Free Press, 1974. Print.

Tannenbaum, R, WH Schmidt. *How to choose a leadership pattern*. Boston: Harvard Business Review, 1973

"The Difference Between Christian and Secular Leadership." Web. 18 June 2014. <https://naturalchurch.wordpress.com/.../the-difference-between-christian-and-secular-l.>

Thompson, Gregg. "Bluepoint Leadership Development." Web. 5 Dec. 2013. <www.bluepointleadership.com/team-member/gregg-thompson/>

Webber, Malcolm. *SpiritBuilt Leadership*. IN: Strategic Press, 2008. Print

www.ingramcontent.com/pod-product-compliance
Lightning Source LLC
Chambersburg PA
CBHW060401080526
44583CB00012B/425